radical
LIBRARY OC
lace
&
subversive
knitting

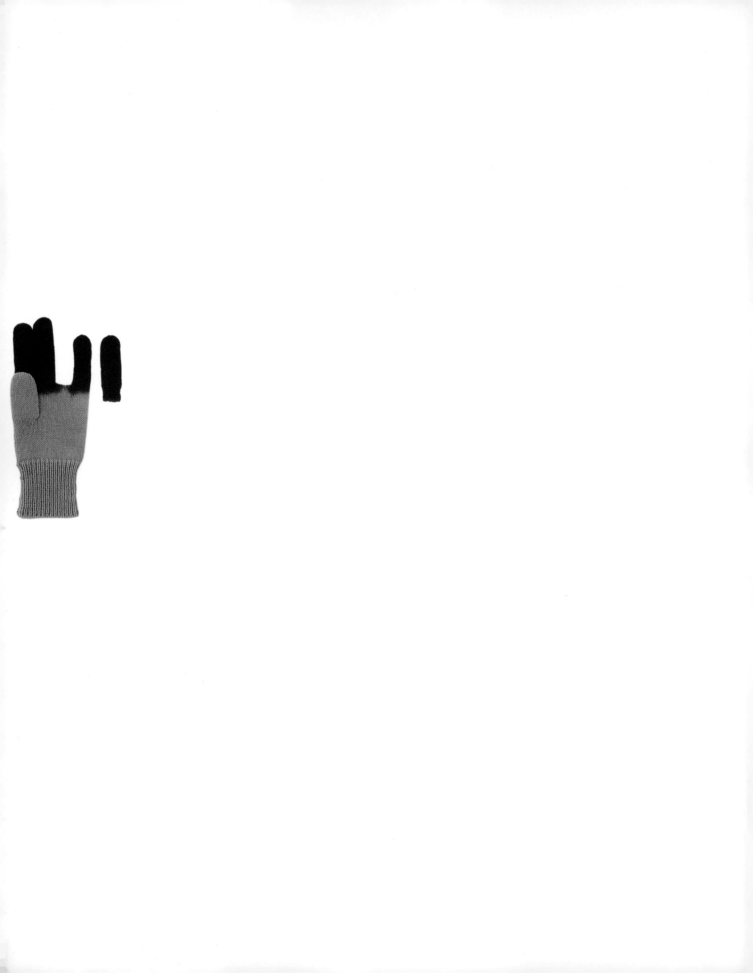

radical lace & subversive knitting

process+materials[1]

David Revere McFadden

with
Jennifer Scanlan
Jennifer Steifle Edwards

ACC EDITIONS   museum of arts and design

Museum of Arts & Design
40 West 53rd Street
New York, New York 10019

First published in conjunction with the exhibition
Radical Lace & Subversive Knitting organized by
the Museum of Arts & Design.

© 2007 Museum of Arts & Design
Reprinted 2008
© 2008 Museum of Arts & Design/
Antique Collectors' Club/ACC Editions
Woodbridge, Suffolk, England

Unless otherwise noted, all the artist's statements quoted
in the texts on pages 22–136 are from interviews
conducted by the authors in August and September 2006.

Radical Lace & Subversive Knitting has been made
possible by grants from the Coby Foundation,
 Coats & Clark, Greenwall Foundation, and Friends
of Fiber Art International. Additional support has
been provided by Brooklace, Inc.; Prym Consumer;
Stork Prints, B.V.; and University of Central England.

Media sponsor: **VOGUEknitting**

Library of Congress Control Number: 2006939069

ISBN 978-1-85149-568-9

Designed by Linda Florio/Florio Design
Edited by Stephen Robert Frankel
Printed and bound in China

FRONT COVER: Cal Lane, *Covered*, 2005 (detail). Sifted soil
on person; dimensions variable. Collection of the artist;
courtesy Foley Gallery, New York

BACK COVER: Dave Cole, *Knit Lead Teddy Bear*, 2006
(see page 58)

FRONTISPIECE: Freddie Robins, *Peggy*, 1997.
Machine knitted wool; 9 1/2 x 6 1/4 in. (24 x 16 cm).
Private collection

OPPOSITE: Cat Mazza, *Knitoscope Screen Shot III*, 2006
(detail; see page 84)

Contents

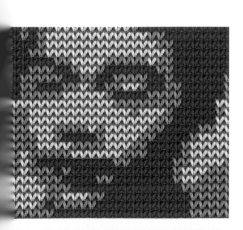

Radical Lace & Subversive Knitting presents a sampling of works that reflect the energy, vitality, and innovation demonstrated by a diverse group of contemporary artists who apply traditional knitting and lacemaking techniques to unusual materials, or new techniques and technologies to traditional materials. The works brought together here, many created specifically for this exhibition, are by artists from seven countries. Individually, these works speak to pervasive and persuasive cultural, social, and political issues with which art intersects today. The role of hand work as a symbol of community and communication is highlighted in many of these pieces, and the artist's personal commitment to collaborative experiments is the focus of others. The works are also barometers of change in the visual arts of our time, signaling the dissolving of the categories of art, craft, and design that have fragmented the world of aesthetic and functional objects for more than a century.

For the Museum of Arts & Design, this exhibition is a wonderful opportunity to share with our international audience the Museum's enhanced and expanded mission to explore and reveal the engagement with materials and process that forms the core of creativity in the visual arts. These artists have thoroughly investigated the limitless potential of the materials and processes associated with the techniques of knitting, crocheting, and lace making, and share those investigations with us through works that are inspiring, whimsical, provocative or meditative. As such, the works acknowledge and honor processes that have been part of human culture for centuries, while looking forward to a future of continuing creative experimentation.

Holly Hotchner
Director

Acknowledgments

Radical Lace & Subversive Knitting could not have been realized without the expert assistance of many colleagues. Curatorial assistant Jennifer Steifle Edwards has been indispensable in coordinating both the exhibition and the accompanying publication, and assistant curator Jennifer Scanlan was her ally in all aspects of both projects. Artist consultant Sabrina Gschwandtner shared her expertise and enthusiasm throughout the planning stages of the exhibition, catalogue, and educational programs. Exhibitions curator Dorothy Globus and installation designer Todd Zwigard have created a memorable and innovative setting for the works and installations. The registrar Linda Clous and associate registrar Megan Krol worked with diplomacy and skill to bring the art works and the artists safely to New York. Meave Hamill and Christina Bachler, curatorial interns, provided invaluable assistance in assembling documentation and images for the project. And, it was the expertise of editor Stephen Robert Frankel and designer Linda Florio that resulted in such a handsome publication.

Lastly, and most importantly, the Museum of Arts & Design extends its sincere thanks to all of the artists who have participated in bringing *Radical Lace & Subversive Knitting* to life by sharing their talents with our public.

David Revere McFadden
Chief Curator, Museum of Arts & Design

Knitting and Lace: Radical and Subversive?

David Revere McFadden

"You knit with great skill, madame."
"I am accustomed to it."
"A pretty pattern too!"
"YOU think so?" said madame, looking at him with a smile.
"Decidedly. May one ask what it is for?"
"Pastime," said madame, still looking at him with a smile while her fingers moved nimbly.
"Not for use?"
"That depends. I may find a use for it one day. If I do— Well," said madame, drawing a
  breath and nodding her head with a stern kind of coquetry, "I'll use it!"

—conversation with Madame Defarge, in Chapter 22 of
    A Tale of Two Cities by Charles Dickens (1859)[1]

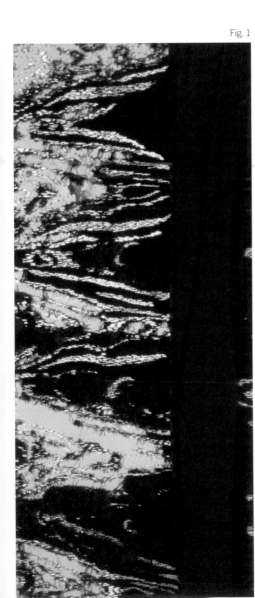

Fig. 1

How does something as innocent and harmless as knitting become subversive? How can lace serve radical ends?

Contemporary artists engaged with materials and process have particularly enjoyed the spotlight in the contemporary-art arena of late. Materials identified with the craft traditions—wood, clay, and, especially, fiber—and the techniques used in their transformation from mute to mutational are today serving the artistic goals of a burgeoning generation of practitioners. Wood turners and carvers, potters and sculptors, knitters, lacemakers, and crochet virtuosi are in the forefront of creativity. In the space of ten years, knitting has emerged from the "loving hands at home" hobbyist's den into museums and galleries worldwide. Knitting clubs meet in cities from San Francisco to Stockholm, while interactive knitting "performances" have been held in seemingly unlikely places such as the London Tube and an abandoned warehouse. Lace has been entirely transformed from being just an accoutrement in the world of effete or erotic fashion into architectural installations and massive sculptures. If the essence of being subversive is to overthrow the status quo from the inside out, these radical reformers in the world of knitting and lace making have succeeded.

As Madame Defarge states, a skill becomes useful when and where it is needed to effect revolutionary change. While she used knitting to record the names of those doomed to be beheaded at the guillotine, a considerable number of today's artists exploit the rich artistic potential of knitting and lace in a deliberate effort to make art that is, in many respects, unlike most of the precedents familiar to them.

This renaissance of interest and activity in knitting and lace structures has been nourished by larger changes in the ways that art is made and perceived. First and foremost has been a re-valuation of hand making as a means of recapturing the sensuality and tactility of sculpture. In a world where the clinical and impersonal nature of digital technologies may perplex and discourage us (and where we daily confront what often seems like the homogeneous anonymity of the global village), what can restore our connection to community, to our history, and to our shared aspirations is the sense of hand—i.e., of making something from start to finish by manual labor. It is not surprising that the reappearance of knitting and other so-called "domestic" handcrafts followed soon after the events of September 11, 2001, establishing new communities of support. Certain aspects of the revival have

Fig. 2

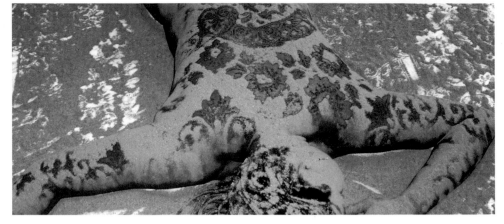

produced noteworthy charity craft events, ranging from the knitting of scarves and hats sold at benefit auctions to the knitting of sweaters for oil-spill–damaged penguins to wear in Antarctica. At the other end of the spectrum has been the emergence of celebrity knitters, both male and female, from the realms of popular culture and entertainment.

Radical Lace & Subversive Knitting looks at a third group of practitioners—sculptors who use the techniques of knitting (creating structures from a single continuous yarn) or the concepts of lace making (creating interlocking structures in patterns that permit light to pass through them). The exhibition includes work by artists from around the world. The works take the form of freestanding sculptures, architectural interventions, sound and video works, and performance art. Here, traditional definitions of materials and techniques that defined both knitting and lace making for centuries are suspended; these works reflect more generous and fluid definitions within a much broader and more inclusive definition of art, no longer concerned with the hierarchies and value systems that separate art from craft and design. The artists and the works selected for *Radical Lace & Subversive Knitting* do not readily fall into any neat classification within that traditional triad of categories—indeed, they challenge stereotypical expectations of knitting or lace making.

This exhibition is concerned with a specific type of material that, for good or for bad, is most commonly referred to as fiber. Coming to mind immediately are those fibers we encounter on a daily basis—cotton, wool, silk, linen, or even polyester—the ones

traditionally identified with the fields of both knitting and lace making. For the purposes of this exhibition, however, "fiber" is greatly expanded to include a wide range of materials that can be manipulated to create knotted or linked structures. In addition to traditional materials, these artists work with rubber, found objects, glass, industrial shelving, wire, and fiber optics.

Materials and techniques serve the needs of artists as a result of intention and choice, not by happenstance or accident. The making of art is dependent on a series of choices as to how and when to utilize a specific material, and how best to transform material—to give it form—through specific behaviors and actions. The mission of the Museum of Arts & Design is to understand and reveal this intentionality, and to celebrate the unique intersection of intelligence, visual acuity, and skill that artists bring to the behavior of making things of aesthetic value. The artists whose work is highlighted in *Radical Lace & Subversive Knitting* are exemplars of this creative process.

This exhibition makes no attempt to define either knitting or lace in any specific historical or technical sense. The history of the two techniques is extraneous to the purpose of the exhibition, even though many of the practitioners highlighted have studied the history of their chosen field in depth, and have learned greatly from those studies. The origins of various knotting and weaving techniques can be traced to prehistory; hand knitting as we know it today is thought to have been in practice as early as the twelfth century, as sites in Islamic Egypt have revealed. By the fourteenth century, paintings of the Virgin Mary sometimes show

her knitting; some of the earliest surviving knitted garments, such as gloves, were produced for liturgical purposes. By the sixteenth century, lace was being produced in abundance, nearly always for an exclusive and moneyed clientele who could afford such grand and expensive embellishments.

Techniques and traditions of the fiber arts have continued to serve the artistic needs of artists over the centuries. One need only glance at the history of the Arts and Crafts Movement of the late nineteenth and early twentieth centuries to find evidence of the vitality of needlework and weaving in the era. Textiles and other fiber-based crafts were included in the curriculum at the Bauhaus, even though they were generally overshadowed by metalwork, ceramics, and furniture design. This exhibition is not primarily about emphasizing the value of handcraft as a cultural and political practice; that point has been driven home in the past decade by numerous exhibitions and publications on the subject. Neither is it simply about revaluing "women's work" and the work of men who perform "women's work" within the contemporary art scene, nor is it about obsessive behaviors manifested in works of art founded in handcraft practices, another popular theme in art writing over the past few years. *Radical Lace & Subversive Knitting* acknowledges the continual revaluation of fiber as a valid medium for art

Fig. 1: Elana Herzog, *Untitled #1*, 2000 (detail). Brocade bedspread, staples, gypsum on plywood panel; 6 ft. 5 in. x 9 ft. 3 in. x 3 in. (2 m x 2.8 m x 7.6 cm). Collection of the artist

Fig. 2: Cal Lane, *Covered*, 2005 (detail). Sifted soil on person; dimensions variable. Collection of the artist; courtesy Foley Gallery, New York

Fig. 3

Fig. 4

Fig. 5

Fig. 3: Liz Collins, *Woodnymph Dress*, 2000. Rayon, mohair, merino wool, silk; dimensions variable. Collection of Kara Walker

Fig. 4: Freddie Robins, *Anyway*, 2002 (detail, see page 28)

Fig. 5: Erna van Sambeek, *Turkish-Dutch Tulip Carpet*, 2004 (detail, see page 32)

throughout the twentieth century, including the pioneering efforts to bring textiles and other fiber-based techniques into the mainstream by such luminaries as Hannah Höch, Sophie Taeuber, and Sonia Delaunay in the early decades of the century, and continuing in the 1960s and '70s as a sculptural and painterly medium by Lenore Tawney, Magdalena Abakanowicz, and Judy Chicago. However, this exhibition is not a retrospective history; that is the subject of a future exhibition.

The forty-two works chosen for this show are indicative of contemporary creative energy in knitting and constructed fiber around the world—by male and female artists of widely different ages who were born or who work in Australia, Brazil, France, Iceland, Japan, the Netherlands, the United Kingdom, or the United States. What unites the diverse works in this exhibition is the implication that both

knitting and lace suggest a delicate domesticity that is belied by the imposing sculptural scale they may assume, by the engaging and even perplexing complexity of their construction, and by their often radical content, which may range from political manifesto to autobiographical revelation.

In mathematics, beauty is often aligned with simplicity; the "elegant" mathematical formula is that which contains the greatest amount of information while utilizing the fewest terms. Purity and simplicity of form often define the salient aspect of beauty in the world of created objects. However, there is another side to beauty, one that grows from complexity and the astonishment and awe that complexity can inspire in the viewer. The beauty explored in *Radical Lace & Subversive Knitting* tends to be of the latter variety. Complexity is inherent in the structures that these artists create; knitting, tatting, crocheting all depend on making gestures that connect fiber to itself, and these gestures are usually repetitive in extended sequences. Other than that complexity, however, what do these particular objects have in common with one another, aside from the medium or technique, that contributes to the larger purpose of the exhibition? These commonalities consist of certain affinities in theme, content, or structure that we have highlighted by presenting the works in subgroups within the larger whole. While all significant works of art are susceptible to perennial reinterpretation— and while recognizing that all categorization can be argued as arbitrary—these themes may be useful as doors of entry to a richer understanding of the works' significance.

Fig. 6

There are several works that refer, in one way or another, to the human body, a seemingly logical extension of a primary function of fiber: covering and displaying the human body. Another group of works examines the ways in which scale and size can influence our interpretation and understanding of what we are looking at. The exhibition also features the work of a group of practitioners /activists who have explored ways to expand their engagement with materials and process within an extended community, using performance and participatory artmaking. Other artists explore unorthodox materials regarded as outside of the world of traditional fiber, often using them to make forms traditionally associated with fiber (such as fiber-optic "lace" lamp shades or gigantic industrial-fiber-and-steel "baskets"), in order to radically alter our expectations of how materials behave. While most of the works in the exhibition are primarily about structure and the process of construction, others arrive at their particular content and beauty by subverting the idea of conventional construction, literally deconstructing solid form into lacey forms by piercing, cutting, and shredding. Lastly, there is a body of works that focus on the way in which complexity of form and technique can convey profound visual, emotional, and spiritual content.

Complexity, structure, materials, process, form, and content all join forces in these works to pursue the exploration of beauty through radical and sometimes subversive actions.

Corporeal Constructions

Liz Collins's career as a designer of her own couture line and as a participant in New York runway fashion shows informs her sculptural constructions that explore the relationship between the body and its coverings. Part theatrical costume, part architectural intervention, Collins's forms are fusions between cloth and knitted passages. Knitting permits her to create stretchy, organic veins that hold together the flimsy, filmy material of the garment. These knitted veins suggest, both visually and structurally, the veins that run through our own fragile flesh (p. 23). In Collins's own words, "My work exposes the inner terrain of the body and the surface of the skin, while simultaneously covering and protecting it. The skeletal structure can function for me in a literal fashion, as I make garments that appear to be x-rays of the body." Collins also extends her artistic vision to collaborative performance works, such as *Knitting Nation*, which orchestrates an army of knitters, wearing uniforms designed by Collins, who collectively produce complex machine knitted banners or wearable garments that deal with issues of nationalism, globalism, and community.[2]

Body imagery and references to the body appear frequently in the work of British artist Freddie Robins. Her knitted garments and installations are generally provocative and unsettling, and imbued with political commentary. She has knitted sweaters for individuals with a single arm, and button-up cosies for trees.[3] Robins recognizes the similarities between computer-programming instructions and knitting, in that each depends on translating complicated information into a type of shorthand.[4] Robins has found knitting to be a perfect vehicle for

exploring the blurred areas that exist between contemporary art and traditional handcraft. She teases the viewer's expectations that knitting is about "fireside, cats, and old women," with her knitted full-body suits that can connote either the reassurance and security of protective armor or the stifling and controlling repression of a uniform or burial shroud. In a work titled *Craft Kills*, the knitted body suit is pierced with dozens of sharp knitting needles, suggesting the martyrdom of a knitted Saint Sebastian (p. 29). Robins reminds the viewer that our bodily fears and frailties are barely disguised by a very thin skin of reason and rationality.

Dutch artist Erna van Sambeek has worked in a wide variety of materials and on projects that involve large-scale architectural and urban settings. Most recently, she led a team of four Muslim women in the design of an enormous public "carpet" of flowering tulips, installed in East Park in Amsterdam in 2006 (p. 32). The social contexts of lace making and knitting are explored by this artist in works that often have a direct political point of view. For this exhibition, van Sambeek has knitted "body warmers" for a homeless family (p. 33). They are knitted from paper, a telling choice due to the impermanence and "worthlessness" of the medium, but, ironically not just any paper, but pages from the distinguished *Financial Times* of London and its Dutch equivalent, *Financieel Dagblad*.

Fig. 6
Yoshiki Hishinuma (installation view of the exhibition *Yoshiki Hishinuma 3d-Knit* at AXIS Gallery, Tokyo, Japan, 2005)

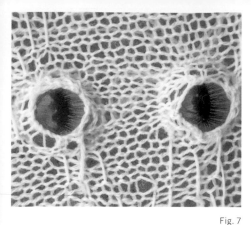

Fig. 7

Fig. 8

Fig. 9

Japanese fashion designer and textile innovator Yoshiki Hishinuma makes use of many new technologies and materials in the design and execution of his extraordinary wearable pieces. For a time, he worked in the studio of the legendary Issey Miyake, but soon went on to begin his own fashion label. Hishinuma has made particular use of new, programmable knitting machines that enable him to create shapes and colors of astonishing complexity and three-dimensionality. Many of these works are inspired by forms from nature—specifically, exotic flowers with unusual colors and textures (pp. 35–37). With his knitting machines, he can translate the subtleties of shape and color into seamless overlapping and fully dimensional knitted garments.

The body is scrutinized in surprising detail by Barbara Zucker, specifically the complexities of wrinkle patterns on her own face and that of others. Zucker takes these patterns and magnifies them to the point of abstraction in works made of steel, aluminum, or vulcanized rubber. Her focus on wrinkles began more than ten years ago as she confronted her own aging and the combination of resignation and resentment that she felt as she observed herself in the mirror.[5] In this exhibition, Zucker's powerful commentary on time, wrinkles, and contemporary social values is seen in *Lilian's Face Flowing*, 2005, a large lace waterfall of black rubber based on the facial wrinkles of a friend (p. 39). In *Lilian on the Floor*, 2001–5, the black lace resembles a pile of castoff black lingerie, with inevitable erotic undertones; and then, viewed as a study of aging flesh, it resonates with the tension between what is perceived and what is known.

It is impossible not to be aware of knitting whenever one dons a sweater; sweaters afford comforting warmth, and the knitted garment allows the fabric to follow the shape of the torso, shrinking and stretching to become a virtual second skin. Ruth Marshall, although she does not directly refer to the human body in her works, uses knitting to elicit a visceral tactile response to the animal bodies she presents. Instead of knitting sweaters, though, Marshall knits life-size replicas of animal skins, as in her *Coral Snake Series*, 2006, featuring knitted-wool snake skins of nearly every variety of one poisonous species (p. 43). Initially, from a distance, viewers are drawn to the bold stripes of black, red, and yellow; and when they get closer, they can appreciate the knitted structure and the subtlety of patterning that the artist has captured. Up close, however, they are also reminded of the implied danger of proximity to a dangerous reptile. Marshall recently commented that often these snakes are rare and endangered; numerous species have not been photographed or studied in depth. Between 1985 and 2005, thirteen new species have been discovered or reclassified. "Why, I ask myself, in this new 21st century, gripped by the 'old' cold fact of habitat loss and species decline do I feel an almost romantic urge to try and say new things about a disappearing world of which there is so much to discover?"[6] Marshall thus adds another layer of discomfort to the experience of attraction /repulsion to the snakeskin image.

Fig. 10

Fig. 7: Ruth Marshall, *Lacey Rocky*, 2005 (detail; see page 45)

Fig. 8: Barbara Zucker, *Inuit Woman*, 2005 (detail; see page 41)

Fig. 9: Annet Couwenberg, *Act Normal and That's Already Crazy Enough*, 2003 (detail; see page 50)

Fig. 10: Janet Echelman, *Roadside Shrine I: Cone Ridge*, 2000 (installation view, Houston, Texas). Nylon net, metal, wood, and staples affixed to interstate highway overpass with C-clamps; 17 x 9 x 57 ft. (5.2 x 2.7 x 17.4 m). Courtesy Florence Lynch Gallery, New York

Fig.12

Matters of Scale

A very different take on the relationship
of fiber to the body is evident in the work
of Annet Couwenberg, from the Netherlands
and now living in the United States.
Couwenberg has focused on elements of
traditional Dutch dress, such as the stiff
ruffled lace collar so familiar from seven-
teenth-century Dutch portraiture. In her
work, the ruffled collar evokes the social
and religious substructure of Dutch culture:
the collar is an outward symbol of cultural
values, and a signifier of one's place within
that culture. As Couwenberg has said,
clothing is "a metaphor that examines the
precarious balance between the constraints
of social norm and our private desires."
The preciousness and rarity of prized lace
is deliberately diminished in the large-scale
installation work that Couwenberg has created for this exhibition, *Discarded Ruffled
Collar*, 2007 (p. 48): an enormous lace
collar composed of more than eight thousand
ordinary paper lace doilies, which truly
fulfills her description of this costume
component as an "elegant burden."[7] By
means of this artistic strategy, Couwenberg
subverts our ideas of value on several levels:
here, inexpensive disposable paper doilies
are awarded a place of value as an art medium, undercutting the history of high-status
costume accessories.

Janet Echelman specializes in public com-
missions on a grand scale, both permanent
and temporary. Her most recent public work,
carried out in Porto, Portugal, is a massive
500-foot-diameter lace basket suspended
over a traffic circle at the harbor (pp. 54,
55). Echelman constantly surprises her
viewers by the sheer magnitude of her public
sculptures, which contrasts with the delicacy

and intricacy of the construction. In the
Porto project, the complex knotting makes
it possible for the entire work to respond to
passing breezes. The giant red-and-white
basket, made of high-tech industrial materials, gently swells and undulates like an
exotic jellyfish responding to minute changes
in water currents.

Dave Cole works in a wide range of scales,
but is probably best known for two works:
his monumental knitting project and
performance piece using two commercial
backhoes to knit a 35-foot-wide American
flag—*The Knitting Machine* (p.59), commissioned by the Massachusetts Museum of
Contemporary Art (Mass MoCA) in 2005—
and his 14-foot-high *Fiberglass Teddy Bear*
knitted from industrial-grade fiberglass
insulation strips, installed at the De Cordova
Museum of Contemporary Art in 2003 (pp.
56, 57). Playing with our expectations of
scale is second nature to Cole; he also
knitted a teddy bear of normal child-friendly
size out of lead strips (*Knit Lead Teddy Bear*,
2006), thus rendering a usually harmless
and innocent toy nearly unliftable and
potentially hazardous (p. 58). He uses the
complexity of his structures on these scales
to engage the viewer; the actual process of
making them is also important to Cole, who
sees knitting as "obsessive, repetitive work,"
but also as a "trope for work, a metaphor for
every kind of production."[8]

At the opposite end of the scale spectrum is
the work of Althea Merback, whose sweaters,
gloves, and socks are so tiny that they would
seem small even to the Lilliputians on
Jonathan Swift's fictional island. Merback
makes knitting needles from medical wires,
using them to knit items of clothing on a

Fig. 11

ig. 11: Dave Cole, *The Money Dress*, 2006 (detail; see page
8)

ig. 12: Althea Merback, *Ancient Greek Pullover*, 2005
detail; see page 63)

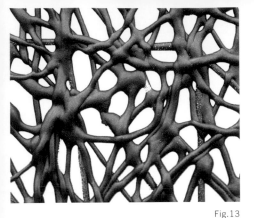
Fig.13

microscopic scale. While one may overlook her work as charming virtuosity, an important point would be missed. Her recent work has included the knitting of a series of highly detailed, minuscule sweaters incorporating imagery from different art-historical periods, including classical Greece, ancient Egypt, and twentieth-century Modernism (specifically, Picasso)—a subtle commentary on the commodification of cultural icons, and steeped with the irony of being works of art that are "unwearable wearables" (pp. 60–63).

Light Constructions

Dutch artist Henk Wolvers is best known for his elegantly deformed ceramic vessels of colored-body porcelains, made by embedding color in paper-thin slabs of porcelain using stains (rather than glazes). Recently, he has carried out experiments in new ways of using porcelain, which can be manipulated not only as a solid, but also as a watery cream-like slurry of clay squeezed through a tube to produce lacelike body walls and large-scale panels of openwork ceramics. What is extraordinary in the panels is the scale at which Wolvers has chosen to work in a medium that is notoriously difficult to fire, especially with unconventional forms. These interwoven porcelain panels resemble lace curtain panels, which, when illuminated, produce wonderful patterns of light and shadow (p. 67).

For well over a decade, artists and designers have experimented with fiber optics. Among the most successful recent designs made with this unusual material are the *Bobbin Lace Lamps* by Niels van Eijk, from the Netherlands (pp.70–73). Van Eijk uses knotted lace techniques to fabricate these enormous hanging chandeliers that consist

Fig.14

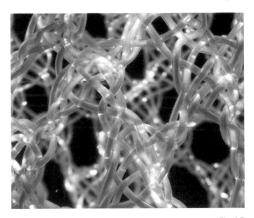
Fig.15

Fig. 13: Henk Wolvers, *Wall Object Study*, 2006 (detail). Porcelain, stain; dimensions variable. Collection of the artist

Fig.14: Bennett Battaile, *History*, 2005 (detail; see page 75)

Fig.15: Niels van Eijk, *Bobbin Lace Lamp*, 2002 (detail; see page 71)

entirely of optical fiber. Van Eijk, who studied craft as well as industrial design, has bridged both worlds in this design, which has the complex structure of knotted lace and, as a result of fiber-optic technology, sparkles with myriad tiny points of light.

Flameworked glass is the medium of choice for Bennett Battaile, who creates lacelike sculptures composed of interlocking threads of clear or colored glass that coruscate with light. Battaile has always had a passion for mathematics, and his background is in software engineering. Working on two-dimensional modeling of mathematical structures soon gave way to making three-dimensional forms using glass threads that could be interwoven into complex lattice structures. In Battaile's intricate constructions, their modest scale (ranging from several inches to just a few feet) is intimately linked to a discriminating sense of proportion; and his inclusion of both clear, transparent glass and opaque black threads in some of these fragile, lacelike pieces gives them a calligraphic presence.

Interconnections

Two artists who use materials and techniques in unexpected ways and with complex layerings of social and cultural meaning are Sabrina Gschwandtner and Cat Mazza. Gschwandtner, founder of *KnitKnit* magazine, has expanded her repertoire of materials to include an enormous variety of natural and synthetic fibers—and sometimes photography and video—to create installations, performance pieces, and freestanding objects. Gschwandtner investigates the potential of knitting, crocheting, and sewing to create connections among individuals, and to create a sense of community. The work she has created for this exhibition is a

Fig.16

Fig.17

handmade book that is to be assembled during the run of the show, incorporating elements made by participants in a "knitting circle" at the Museum. This will become a living record of interactions generated through shared interests in process.

Mazza, founder of microRevolt, has created a series of art projects that combine knitting, digital technologies, and politics in a distinctive manner. Mazza's focus on raising consciousness about manufacturing processes in sweatshops around the world has been the impetus for large-scale community knitting projects to protest exploitation of labor. Best known is her 14-foot-wide blanket depicting the Nike "swoosh," constructed of hundreds of individually knitted squares made by participants from many countries (p. 86). Adding another layer of complexity to the social mandate she has set herself in her knitting practice, Mazza created a software program called knitPro, which translates a still or moving image directly into patterns for knitting, crocheting, or needlework. The software can be used without cost by anyone, a radical decision that underscores her commitment to communal goals and ideals.

The communal nature of knitting is also central to the work of Françoise Dupré, one of the few knitting artists who uses an old-fashioned knitting spool rather than standard needles. Using this simple tool, Dupré fabricates lengths of tubular knit cords, which she arranges to form various kinds of compositions, such as round, targetlike color and texture studies attached to walls (as in French Knitting, 2003, p. 90), and larger floor targets surrounded by looped, stylized flowers or snowflakes made with the same material. She has specialized in organizing

knitting interventions, sometimes with unskilled participants, who jointly design and fabricate the final work with her. Dupré is inspired by theorist and historian Michel de Certeau's concept of art making in the everyday; she says, "My work aims to celebrate the vernacular and creative skills that are invisible, marginal, or being lost through migration, socio-economic changes, and globalization."[9]

Shane Waltener has established an art-making practice that consists of both his own individual interventions in various public and private buildings, and community-based collaborations with groups of people in knitting-based performances. Waltener is known for his guerilla knitting projects that leave behind knotted-fiber spider webs in unexpected venues such as commercial storefronts or abandoned buildings. One of the most dramatic of these interventions in public settings was a giant cobweb installed in the grand lobby of the Victoria and Albert Museum in London—a sly, irreverent comment on the museum as a tomb for cultural artifacts (pp. 92, 93). Waltener's community-based projects have included outdoor knitting festivals that engage casual passersby in a group art project, in which they all work on a single large piece.

Fig.18

Fig.19

Fig.16: Sabrina Gschwandtner, video still from *The KnitKnit Sundown Salon*, 2004 (video, 6 mins. 36 secs.). Bergen National Academy of the Arts, Norway

Fig.17: Cat Mazza, *Nike Petition Blanket* workshop at 3Walls Gallery, Chicago, Illinois, 2006

Fig.18: Shane Waltener, *Knitting Piece #13*, 2006 (performance at South Hill Park, Bracknell, England). People knitting, wool, circular needles, hay bales, tent pegs; dimensions variable

Fig.19: Françoise Dupré, *Fujaan*, 2005 (detail, see page 91)

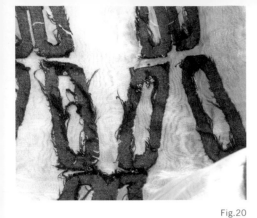

Fig.20

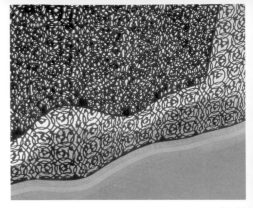

Fig.24

Fig. 21

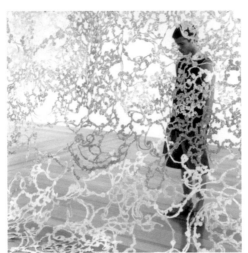

Fig.23

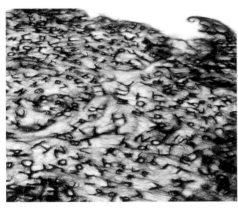

Fig.22

Creative Deconstructions

Both knitting and lace making are constructive processes in which strands of fiber are interwoven or knotted to create structure and to define space. Lace, in its broadest definition, is any fiber construction that allows light to pass freely through it, a criterion articulated in an exhibition entitled *Holes Surrounded by Thread*.[10] The effect is one that can be achieved through a wide variety of construction techniques, but also by deconstructing whole cloth.

Cal Lane transforms mundane found objects, often of an industrial nature, into lace fantasies. Lane has developed the technique of torch-cutting metal to an extraordinary degree, and has used the process to create lacey garden spades, wheelbarrows, dumpsters, and even steel I-beams. Inherent in the work is an ironic recognition that lace is primarily defined as a feminine accessory to dress. Lane's lace sculptures are quintessentially masculine forms completely penetrated

by the feminine—a clever and insightful role reversal that requires viewers to rethink stereotypes and conventional expectations.

Piper Shepard creates large-scale panels of openwork that often resemble specific historical lace patterns that were originally made by knotting individual threads. Her subversive gesture is to cut similar patterns out of whole cloth. Beginning with a plain tightly woven fabric that is impregnated with a gesso-like coating, then sprayed with commercial-grade graphite, she uses an X-acto knife to cut each tiny fragment of cloth away from the ground to create the complex patterns. When suspended vertically in a room, these panels interact with ambient light to produce an almost gauzelike screen. Shepard, deeply engaged with process in the creation of these lace panels, emphasizes that textile-making is essentially about "repetition, accumulation, and perseverance."[11]

The poetry of deconstruction is central to the work of Brooklyn-based Elana Herzog. She has long used the medium of fabrics—often found objects—to create installations that capture and reveal time and decay in particularly memorable ways. Herzog begins by attaching a textile, such as an old-fashioned or vintage chenille bedspread, to a sheetrock panel using thousands of industrial staples. She then partially deconstructs both the textile and the network of staples, resulting in a haunting ghostlike image of what was once whole cloth. Tatters of fabric hang from the wall and move in the breeze, but they are ultimately—and permanently—held prisoner by the staples.

Deconstruction is among an array of techniques that textile designer Eugène van

Fig. 25

Veldhoven of the Netherlands uses to develop prototypes for the textile industries. Van Veldhoven constantly experiments with new digital, mechanical, and chemical processes that alter the appearance of flat fabrics. For some of his recent prototypes, he has employed these elaborate processes to create unusual textures, or hanging strips, or holes in discrete areas of the fabric—processes such as burn-out (a chemical process that dissolves the cellulose and leaves other fibers intact) and laser cutting (an industrial process that melts, burns, or evaporates material by directing the output of a high-powered laser in a pre-programmed path).

The Beauty of Complexity

The artists highlighted in *Radical Lace & Subversive Knitting* are all engaged in a dialogue with structure and process, material and meaning. To varying degrees and for different reasons, they have chosen their mediums and transformed them through particular processes to create something that is somehow larger than the sum of its parts, its knots, its knits and purls. More than a few of them use fiber in ways that resonate with the connections between making art and writing texts. In many instances, the fiber becomes a dimensional equivalent to a drawn line or written phrase; it is manipulated to reflect an inner logic and syntax by the artist, and yet remains a complex post-literate series of lines and curves in space.

Hildur Bjarnadóttir uses knitting, crocheting, and tatting in her work, drawing on the historical and cultural matrix that made these techniques so important in her native Iceland. Her art engages attention through patterns that may appear highly traditional at first glance, but which reveal themselves to

be entirely contemporary in content, as in *Untitled (Skulls)*, 1999, which combines a somewhat off-kilter arrangement of doily-like lace forms with a border of crocheted skulls: the quaint and cozy world of crocheted table doilies and antimaccassars suddenly reveals a much darker aspect (pp. 116, 117). Bjarnadóttir is represented in this exhibition by a large tatted wall sculpture (p. 119). The work is dyed a brilliant blue obtained by using fountain-pen ink. This choice of dyestuff underscores Bjarnadóttir's concept that she is literally "writing with thread" in her works, keeping a journal of time and place with each series of intricate and diminutive knots that define the technique.[12] Her knotted "doodles" are like illegible or "invented" cursive writing, or suggestive of a wayward road map, with its convoluted twists and turns. Simultaneously, they often resemble passages of lace removed from a vintage tablecloth and reconfigured as an ornamental construction that refers to itself alone. The works are complex in their fabrication, and multilayered in their historical and contemporary meaning.

An equally rich historical vein of imagery is mined by Carson Fox in her knotted panels of scrollwork fabricated of wire and synthetic hair. These filigree wall pieces resemble antique wrought-iron gates or fences, and also mementos that Victorians made out of the hair of their dear departed. Fox's work, like that of Bjarnadóttir, is all about line and "drawing in space." One piece, *I Know About Your Broken Heart*, 2004, extends the delineation of line into written words—an incantation of a single phrase, repeated over and over (p. 123). The use of hair and fine wire makes these lacey panels unusually transparent; the shadows that they produce

on the wall look every bit as substantial as the actual piece, hinting at the fragility of memory and the illusions about permanence that we depend on in our lives.

Writing in thread is an apt metaphor for the installations of Brazilian artist Hilal Sami Hilal. Using cotton fibers and metallic oxides, Hilal creates structures that are as visually light as air, but with the rich patination that comes only with the passing of time and the interaction of the elements. A frequent motif in Hilal's work is the book, which he presents as a series of calligraphic tangible gestures bound together as lacey pages. Like fragments of an ancient and indecipherable scroll, these works are evidence of a human presence. His hanging panels, such as the one included in this exhibition, suggest once-living plants and foliage found pressed in some long-forgotten volume, discolored with time and age, but still redolent with nostalgia (pp. 126, 127).

Edward Mayer taps into the potential magic to be revealed in humble, everyday objects in his architectural interventions composed of commercial vinyl shelving, gardening-center plant cages and trellises, and found branches or other natural detritus. Like a shaman releasing the power of an inanimate object, Mayer assembles such elements into an apparently fragile structure, creating a complex realm in which the boundaries between substance and nothingness fade. His installations make use of the interplay of line and light to an unusual degree. All the objects are white (or covered with white tape), which focuses the viewer's attention on the relationships between individual

Fig. 25: Edward Mayer, *Drawing In*, 2005 (see page 129)

Fig. 26   Fig. 27

elements and the whole. The complex inter-weaving of linear elements creates visual planes and volumes, but volumes possessing an ephemeral beauty, like that of an orchard of leafless trees or a cluster of telephone poles and wires transformed by a winter snowfall.

Sheila Pepe knots, crochets, and weaves within an architectural context, employing a palette of materials that range from shoelaces and rubber bands to nautical towing line and hardware store rope. Chosen with deliberation and intent, each of these materials is embedded with personal and cultural histories that can be revealed through their use: the shoelaces, for example, recall memories of her Italian-born grandfather's shoe-repair stores in Brooklyn. Pepe's complex webs cause the viewer to regard the materials from which they are spun in a new light; the commonplace and ordinary synthetic rope or tow line becomes a passage of line and color, while the elemental knots and twists become their own ornamental embellishments.

Complexity of ideas combined with an exceptional elegance in the creation of complex forms come to a unique point of balance in the work of Anne Wilson. Wilson explores the ways in which inner worlds of perception and meaning are manifested in fragile physical structures. For this artist, experience of the work of art cannot be separated from our sense of time and space. Her geographical landscapes made of fiber can only be comprehended as the viewer moves around the work. Each constellation of elements resolves itself in relation to the whole. Even though the work of art is fixed and static in its composition, it is animated by the viewer's

movement around it and the resulting changing field of vision.

Wilson's recent work has gone beyond the composition of material objects to become the focus of video and sound works, through which her complex and layered landscape of eccentric forms comes to life (p. 137).

What does it mean for the history of knitting and lace making that Wilson has so radically and subversively recast the field of fiber in a new form? How does what she has done with lace give an insight into the larger intent of *Radical Lace & Subversive Knitting*? Video is not a substitute for real experience, nor is it a prosthetic add-on to the tangible world. Wilson reminds us that what is of ultimate value is our experience of the work of art in time and space; that experience is seductively offered in Wilson's magic-lantern chamber.

Materials speak their own language to these artists, as do the techniques that they choose to employ to work with them to achieve their vision. The limitations usually placed on either a material or a technique are insignificant and possibly nonexistent. These artists individually and collectively know that their artistic intentions can only be realized when their engagement with their materials and processes are profound and intense. The result of this engagement can range from a temporary intervention in space to a collaborative enterprise. Each work invites the viewer to reexamine and reconsider how fiber functions on tangible and spiritual levels. At this point of intersection, the final difference between image and meaning has disappeared.

However, the significance of the works in a larger realm lies in the diversity of ways that these artists contribute to the debate about the role of materials and process that is energizing the visual arts today. Over the past two decades, a radical rewriting of contemporary art to embrace a wider variety of mediums than ever before is undeniable. Today, artists working in clay, glass, metal, wood, and fiber are among the most innovative and noteworthy. These mediums have always suffered from an artificial hierarchy that placed "Art" above both craft and design. The erosion of this hierarchy has come about, to a great extent, through the radical and often subversive strategies of contemporary artists who have changed our perceptions and understanding of traditional materials and techniques. The artists whose works are featured in *Radical Lace & Subversive Knitting* have moved the medium of fiber into a new prominence. Taking preconceived notions of what knitting and lace has been and can be, they have started a new and lively dialogue about how and why art is made.

Fig. 26: Sheila Pepe, *Shrink*, 2000 (detail of installation view at Ezra and Cecile Zilkha Gallery, Wesleyan University, Middletown, Connecticut). Rubber bands; dimensions variable

Fig. 27: Anne Wilson, *Microcosm (One)*, 2005 (detail). Lace, thread, pins, wood support; 5 x 40 x 13 in. (12.7 x 101.6 x 33 cm). 21st Century Museum of Contemporary Art, Kanazawa, Japan

NOTES

1. Madame Defarge, one of the major characters in Dickens's novel, knitted continuously while attending meetings of the French Revolutionary assemblies and while watching people being executed by guillotine. She encoded a long list of aristocrats and enemies of the Revolutionary government in the stitches of her knitting.

2. Knitting Nation first performed *Knitting During Wartime* as part of "The Muster," organized in 2005 on Governors Island, New York, with Phase 2 occurring at Felissimo Design House in New York in 2006.

3. To get an idea of the range of Robins's knitted works, see *Cosy: Freddie Robins*, catalogue of an exhibition at Firstsite, Colchester, England, 2002, with an introduction by Katherine Wood.

4. "Both involve a complicated series of moves condensed into arcane shorthand; a false move or dropped stitch along the way can cause both to unravel." Ruth Pavey, "Unwearable Tension," *Crafts Magazine* no. 160 (September/October 1999): 39.

5. For a full artist's statement and an excellent essay by Amy Ingrid Schlegel, see the brochure produced for the *Time Signatures* exhibition at Tufts University Art Gallery, February 10 to March 27, 2005.

6. Marshall, e-mail to the author, May 2006.

7. Couwenberg, in conversation with the author, May 2006.

8. Cole, quoted in Cate McQuaid, "Stars & Stripes & Heavy Machinery," *Boston Globe*, July 1, 2005.

9. Dupré, in conversation with the author, May 2006.

10. *Holes Surrounded by Thread*, Immigration Museum, Melbourne, Australia, March 12 to September 14, 2003.

11. Shepard, in conversation with the author, August 2006.

12. Bjarnadóttir, in conversation with the author, June 2006.

corporeal constructions

liz collins

b. 1968 in Bethesda, Maryland;

lives in Providence, Rhode Island

Education: B.F.A. (textiles) 1991,
M.F.A. (textiles) 1999, Rhode Island
School of Design, Providence

Collins gravitated toward clothing as a means of personal expression at a very early age; at ten, she took her first class in fashion illustration. After explorations "with every possible creative medium that exists in the visual world, [she] came full circle to fashion and textiles." Her early childhood dream of becoming a fashion designer was achieved with the New York City runway premiere of her collection in the fall of 2000. It was knitting that inspired her to get there.

Right after graduating college, Collins learned to hand knit, and was immediately taken with the process: "It readdressed my interests in fashion and textiles, in a really focused way, for the first time since I was a child." With a friend, Collins opened a clothing boutique in Providence, and began hand-knitting wearable products for sale, first in their own store and then to boutiques in New York City. Inspired and motivated by the new work, Collins decided to return to Rhode Island School of Design to develop her knitting skills and to gain in-depth knowledge of contemporary knitting techniques.

After taking classes in machine-knitting, Collins began to challenge the limitations of the technology by pursuing extensive material explorations. This led to her invention of a new technique, which she dubbed "knit grafting." She applies this technique in her work by knitting multiple rows of narrow cords and, once every several rows, attaching a piece of non-knit fabric to the knitting construction so that they "fuse" together. This allows her to sculpt flat fabric into a three-dimensional form using one continuous process: "I get to direct the line, making it thick or thin, wide or narrow. It is painting with knitted yarn, shaping the fabric as I go." Collins has used "knit grafting" for seaming, creating layers, building up forms, and embellishment; the resulting works are extremely diverse, but share the visual evidence of the technique, variously evoking "veins, tree branches, nerve endings, and other structures which have lines that connect, fan off, and get smaller."

To make *Illuminated Veins (after EV)*, 2006, the work she designed for this exhibition, she used her signature technique. The evening gown is based on a classic 1950s silhouette and combines silk organza with knitted "veins" of a reflective synthetic material that extend out from the dress, connect to, and interact with parts of the Museum's architecture. Guided by the shape, and excited by the mode of construction, she has created a piece that not only clearly articulates both material and structure, but also relates to ideas of bondage, wrapping, tension, and relief.

—J.S.E.

ABOVE LEFT: Collins, in one of her collaborative performance works, *KNITTING NATION: Knitting During Wartime*, on Governors Island, New York, 2005

OPPOSITE: *Illuminated Veins (after EV)*, 2006 (detail)

BELOW: *Illuminated Veins (after EV)*, 2006
Silk organza, silk yarn, 3M Scotchlite reflective film
Dimensions variable
Collection of the artist

Sock Monkey Bikini, 2003 (modeled during the
showing of Collins's fall 2003 collection)
Cashmere, merino wool
Dimensions variable
Collection of the artist

T: *Pride*, 2002 (in collaboration with designer Gary
[nam]) Vintage flags and nylon mesh, machine-knitted
[le]ather and embellished with knit wool
[dime]nsions variable
[Colle]ction of the artist

[Belo]w: *Vein Bustier*, 2005 (detail)
[cotto]n, wool, rayon, plastic-wrapped cotton cord
[24 x]36 in. (61 x 91.4 cm)
[RISD] Museum Costume and Textiles Collection, donated
[by B]arnaby Evans and Irene Lawrence

freddie robins

b. 1965 Hitchin, Hertfordshire, England; lives in London

Education: B.A. (constructed textiles), 1987, Middlesex Polytechnic, London; M.A. (textile design), 1989, Royal College of Art, London

For Robins, knitting has always been associated with the contemporary and the cutting edge. Robins grew up in Brighton, England, during the 1970s and early '80s, a period in which knitting was a popular outlet for creativity. Looking back on that time, she noted: "I never associated sewing and knitting with things that were frumpy, with old ladies. I always thought of it as something fashionable. It was only later that I realized it had all of these stigmas."

Robins has focused her artwork on undermining these associations and stigmas, mocking them with playful humor. For example, she knitted *Tree Cosies*—the title is a pun (verbal and conceptual) on "tea cosies"—to cover trees in an installation she created for a group show called *The Garden pARTy* in 1997.

The two works by Robins presented in this exhibition deliberately play against stereotypes of knitting as comfortable, non-confrontational, and happily domestic, instead using dark humor that can instill a sense of discomfort even as it makes us laugh. *It Sucks*, 2005, is a hand-knit shawl made of delicate Shetland lace, based on a traditional Shetland christening shawl, but with the rude slogan "IT SUCKS" knitted into it. "It's a real comment on motherhood and babies, and on knitting as well, thinking of the Shetland women knitting these shawls for a living. It just sucks, if

you are having to do it for money continuously." *Craft Kills*, 2002, is a self-portrait of the artist as St. Sebastian, being martyred by knitting needles instead of arrows—a work composed of machine-knitted wool and actual knitting needles. "It's a real play on how people see craft and textiles, and particularly knitting, as a very passive activity. I'm interested in how would it be if knitting were seen as something very violent or something you weren't allowed to do. Ironically, shortly after I made that piece, knitting needles were banned on aircraft."

Parallel to her interest in the hand-knitted object and its associated values, Robins explores the connections between technology and knitting. In 1999, she was commissioned by inIVA (International Institute for Visual Arts) to create an experimental Web site that linked knitting to computing and the internet (www.iniva.org/xspaceprojects/robins). The site enables users to make nonsensical, multi-sleeved garments with graphic designs based on knitted patterns, experiments that led to Robins's work *Anyway*, 2002, a series of four-sleeved sweaters knit together by machine to form a honeycomb. These large machine-made works succeed in subverting conventional ideas about the knitted object.

—J.S.

ABOVE LEFT: Robins in her studio in London, 2001

BELOW: *Tree Cosies*, 1997 (installation view of *The Garden pARTy (Feeringbury VII)*, Feering, Essex, England Machine- and hand-knitted mohair wool, buttons (hand-knitting by Molly Robins)

It Sucks, 2005
Wool (hand-knitted by Audrey Yates)
39 1/2 x 39 1/2 in. (100 x 100 cm)
Collection of the artist

Anyway, 2002
Machine-knitted wool
5 1/2 x 10 x 10 ft. (1.7 x 3 x 3 m)
Castle Museum, Nottingham, England; purchased by the
 Contemporary Art Society, London

Kills, 2002
...ine-knitted wool, knitting needles
...³⁄₄ in. x 26 ³⁄₄ in. x 15 in. (2m x 68 cm x 38 cm)
...ction of the artist

erna van sambeek

b. 1956 in Texel, the Netherlands; lives in Amsterdam

Education: Studied painting and printmaking, 1990, Gerrit Rietveld Academy, Amsterdam

Van Sambeek's initial studies were in painting, but she found shortly after graduation that the medium stifled her creativity. She searched for another medium that would restore her joy in art-making and eventually turned to textiles, which she had loved as a child. Textiles have become a "trigger," as van Sambeek says, for the conceptualization process that is the basis of all her art. "I like working out an idea. Once I start a piece, the whole plan is already made; I know what the material will be, I know what the idea will be, and then there is only executing it." She does the planning verbally, in written notes, rather than visually, with sketches.

Van Sambeek's execution of these ideas often involves fiber-related materials or techniques, as with the pieces by her that are presented in this exhibition. In two of them, as in many of her works, materials take on functions or appearances that contradict the conventional cultural associations we have of them. In *Snow-cover*, 2005, she used felt—a material normally associated with warmth and comfort—to depict snowflakes. *Body Warmers for a Poor Family*, 2006, were knitted out of strips of newspapers, which poor people often use as insulation under their clothing—and van Sambeek has added an ironic twist by choosing the *Financial Times* of London and its Dutch equivalent, *Financieel Dagblad*. Her third work included in this exhibition, *Floral Gown*, 2004, is

a colorful takeoff on floral lace patterns: whereas lace usually relies on form and texture (and little or no color) to depict arrangements of a few different flowers repeated in symmetrical patterns, van Sambeek cut out many different vividly colored flowers from her collection of floral prints to make a non-repeating floral pattern—and left the spaces between the flowers empty, with the white wall showing through.

A work that makes reference to textiles without actually using any is her outdoor installation *Turkish-Dutch Tulip Carpet*, 2004. This piece is based on the interrelationships between Turkey and van Sambeek's native Holland. As a child, she was surprised to discover that the quintessentially Dutch tulips grown by her father actually came from Turkey; and later, while visiting Turkey, she found tulip patterns in some carpets there, giving her the idea to make a carpet out of real tulips. Organized in a public park in a part of Amsterdam that was often the site of racially charged conflict, and designed with the help of four local women from Turkey, the *Turkish-Dutch Tulip Carpet* became a gathering place for residents and a source of discussion as it grew and bloomed over the course of one spring.

—J.S.

ABOVE LEFT: Van Sambeek in her studio in Amsterdam, 2

OPPOSITE: *Snow-cover*, 2005 (detail)
Handmade felt, fiberfill, rayon lining
75 x 50 ¹/₂ in. (190 x 128 cm)
Collection of the artist

BELOW: *Floral Gown*, 2004
Cotton (hand-cut from various found or collected fabrics), textile glue, cotton backing
59 x 47 in. (150 x 119.5 cm)
Collection of the artist

ABOVE: *Floral Gown*, 2004 (detail)
Cotton (hand-cut from various found or collected fabrics),
  textile glue, cotton backing
59 x 47 in. (150 x 119.5 cm)
Collection of the artist

RIGHT: *Turkish-Dutch Tulip Carpet*, 2004 (aerial view and
  detail, installation view in Oosterpark, Amsterdam, 2006)
98 ft. 6 in. x 65 ft. 6 in. (30 x 20 m)

ly Warmers for a Poor Family, 2006
spapers (*Financial Times* and *Financieel Dagblad*)
into 3/8-inch strips and knitted to several sizes
est: approx. 31 1/2 x 26 in. (80 x 66 cm)
ection of the artist

b. 1958, Sendai City, Japan;

lives in Tokyo

Education: Studied, 1977,
Bunka College of Fashion,
Tokyo

Hishinuma began his career as a fashion designer working for Issey Miyake. Shortly thereafter he was awarded the Mainichi Fashion Grand Prix for young talent. Since introducing his own fashion label in 1992, Hishinuma has become an internationally established designer at the forefront of contemporary knitwear innovation. His unique designs utilize new machine-knitting technology that make it possible to knit a three-dimensional form as one continuous piece, from beginning to end. "The process is like making a molded chair—seamless, without cutting material," he says. Also like a chair, Hishinuma's designs are a sculptural and architectural resolution to constructing form that is closely related to the body.

Hishinuma began creating what he termed "3-D clothing" in 1994, using a combination of heat and synthetic fibers to shrink fabric. The process produces results similar to those seen in traditional Japanese *shibori*, where fabric is folded, tied, and submerged in dye to create patterns. For Hishinuma's contemporary version of *shibori*, he wrapped and secured polyester fabric around sculptural wooden forms, then submerged them in boiling water: the intense heat caused the flat cloth to shrink around the forms, preserving their shapes, patterns, and textures in the finished garment. In a variation of the process, he sculpted three-dimensional garments using flat fabric by stitching polyester yarn into the fabric, and applying heat; the yarn then shrinks to 50 percent of its original size, puckering and shaping the fabric into an elastic, flexible garment that conforms to the contours of the body.

To take the concept of "3-D clothing" even further, Hishinuma began working with innovative, computer-controlled, three-dimensional knitwear technology. Using this method, he created *Casablanca*, 2005, included in this exhibition, which was inspired by the organic forms of the Casablanca lily. Hishinuma based his design for this piece on an abstract representation of the flower separated into two parts, the petals and pistil, and developed a pattern that seamlessly replicated the intricate organic forms. "The process of making organic forms with new technology goes beyond Modernism's geometry of squares, circles, and straight lines," he has observed. The level of geometrical ingenuity involved in the design of *Casablanca* is as complex as the production is simple. Each seamless knit design is programmed into a computer interface that controls the operation of the knitting machine, thus fabricating the knitted piece continuously to generate a completed garment.

—J.S.E.

ABOVE LEFT: Hishinuma in his studio in Tokyo, 2005

OPPOSITE: *Spotted Lily*, 2005 (from Hishinuma's autumn-winter 2005 collection)
Wool seamless knitwear
H. 33 1/2 in., W. 39 1/2 in. (85 x 100 cm)

OPPOSITE: *Hibiscus*, 2005 (from Hishinuma's
 autumn-winter 2005 collection)
Wool seamless knitwear
H. 51 in., W. 47 ¼ in. (130 x 120 cm)

Casablanca, 2005 (from Hishinuma's autumn-winter
 2005 collection)
Wool seamless knitwear
H. 27 ½ in., W. 29 ½ in. (70 x 75 cm)

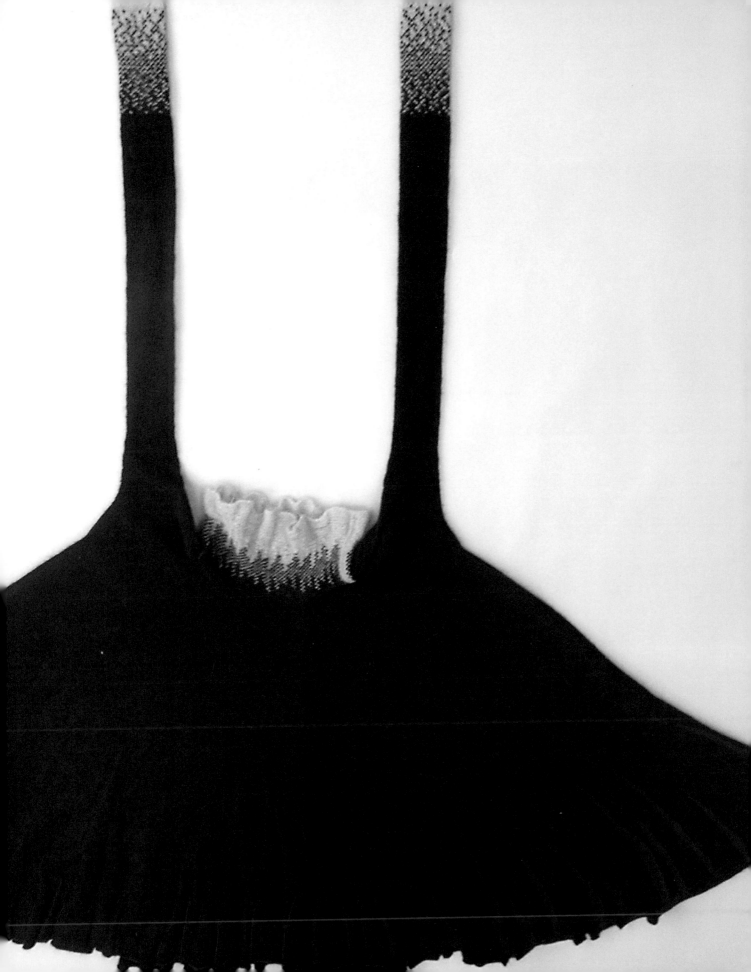

barbara zucker

b. 1940, Philadelphia, Pennsylvania;

lives in Burlington, Vermont

Education: B.S. (design), 1962,
University of Michigan, Ann Arbor;
M.A. (sculpture), Hunter College,
New York

Zucker's *Time Signatures* examine the aging process. These works are abstractions of the intricate patterns formed by the wrinkles on women's faces, transformed into large but delicate sculptural reliefs. Zucker subverts conventional ideas about beauty by turning signs of aging that are considered ugly and undesirable in our youth-obsessed culture into patterns evoking lace, or the branches of rivers or plants.

For much of her artistic career, Zucker has explored culturally imposed notions of female beauty. The *Time Signatures* series grew out of an earlier series of work called *For Beauty's Sake*, a whimsical take on the phenomenon of plastic surgery. Zucker says, "I was younger when I did those pieces, and I thought plastic surgery was amusing; now, everybody on the street can have something lifted, tucked, filled, nipped, changed, altered. As I got older, I realized that getting old wasn't that funny anymore."

In creating her pieces, Zucker starts with images of older women—herself, friends, or well-known women whom she admires—and searches for a striking pattern produced by the wrinkles. This pattern, enlarged and manipulated, becomes the template for the sculpture. Zucker's first pieces were cut out of steel. "In those works, I was trying to take something that was perceived in the culture as a negative and turn it into a very strong positive. Initially, I thought that the hardest and most aggressive material that I could use would be steel."

Eventually she began experimenting with other materials, including aluminum and rubber. She found that rubber gave her the power to manipulate the forms and, in a sense, conquer them symbolically: "I wanted to be able to throw them around or cast them off at will, like pulling the skin away from the face and throwing age on the floor." Zucker used rubber as her medium for *Lilian's Face Flowing*, 2005, which is presented in this exhibition. It features a cascading network of wrinkles that has become a dynamic entity of its own—an enormous veil, or a river.

Zucker's *Inuit Woman*, 2005, a "triptych" cut from sheets of steel, is the largest piece she has done so far, occupying a large expanse on a single wall. Based on a photograph of an Aleutian Island woman that Zucker found in a newspaper, this piece represents a shift in her exploration of the subject of aging. No longer trying to emphasize the abstract beauty of the wrinkle pattern, she has replicated most of the face, and repeated it three times with slight variations. Here, the images are more recognizably faces, and the interlocking patterns of the wrinkles are more tightly woven and dominating. Lace, no longer a symbol of fragile or organic beauty, has become a defiant symbol of power.

—J.S.

ABOVE LEFT: Zucker in her studio with *Inuit Woman* in Burlington, Vermont, 2005

OPPOSITE: *Lilian's Face Flowing*, 2005 (detail)
Rubber
Dimensions variable
Collection of the artist

BELOW: Ken Burris and Barbara Zucker
Lilian, 2001 (photograph of Lilian Baker Carlyle, used as source for *Lilian* sculptures)
Gelatin-silver print
10 x 8 in. (25.4 x 20.3 cm)
Collection of the artist

Rosa Parks, 2001
Steel
31 1/2 x 13 1/2 x 1 1/2 in. (80 x 34.3 x 3.8 cm)
Collection of the artist

ABOVE: *Inuit Woman*, 2005
Water-jet cut steel
Dimensions variable
Collection of the artist

Rear view of *Front of My Neck*, 2006 (detail)
on steel table
20 1/2 x 35 x 20 in. (52.1 x 88.9 x 50.8 cm)
30 x 53 x 29 1/2 in. (76.2 x 134.6 x 74.9 cm)
tion of the artist

ruth marshall

Marshall's reverence and respect for animals permeates her life in many ways. She spends her days at the Bronx Zoo in New York City as an exhibit sculptor, replicating natural habitats for the resident animals and creating educational tools for visitors.

Encountering exotic, wild animals is commonplace for Marshall; so is knitting. When Marshall was working to re-create a Congo gorilla forest at the zoo, a colleague noticed her fascination with the skin patterns of a Gabon viper and jokingly suggested she knit it. Marshall was intrigued by the idea of knitting animal skins, and since then has analyzed, studied, and—using knitting needles and yarn—replicated the skins of numerous kinds of animals.

What interested Marshall most was that she was attracted to the animals for the same reasons that a hunter would be — because "the initial response has to do with the impact of the animal itself and just how beautiful, exotic or different it is." She sees her work as a positive alternative to hunting. "People desire animal skins. My thinking about it is: Why can't you desire something that has been inspired by the animal skin instead? It is a much more inventive and creative way to preserve the animals, and also embodies the idea of desiring something, of possession."

For *Rocky Rug*, 2005, Marshall used her pet cat as a model, and tried to knit the most accurate representation possible. After many fruitless attempts to have Rocky sit still for measurements, Marshall took her cat to the veterinarian to get his teeth cleaned, and, while he was still anesthetized, took more than 100 photographs and numerous measurements. Even with all this information, it took her more than four weeks to map out the knitting pattern precisely enough to capture his likeness in wool. *Rocky Rug*, which shows the cat in a seemingly lifeless state, provokes us to consider such matters as desire, obsession, and death.

Marshall used a very different conceptual approach for her *Coral Snake Series*, 2006, which is presented in this exhibition. It consists of life-size knitted replicas of nearly every variety of coral snake in the world, to affirm the importance of animal preservation. In this project, she highlights the wide range of color, pattern, and beauty among the various snake skins. The individual identification tags tied to each snake not only document the diversity within this single species, but can also be read as morbid reminders of the perpetual risk of extinction that threatens many species.

—J.S.E.

b. 1964 in Melbourne, Australia; lives in Bronx, New York

Education: B.A. (sculpture), 1991, Phillip Institute of Technology, Bundoora, Melbourne, Australia (now known as Royal Melbourne Institute of Technology); M.F.A., 1995, Pratt Institute, Brooklyn, New York

ABOVE LEFT: Marshall in her studio in Bronx, New York, 20

OPPOSITE: *Coral Snake Series*, 2006 (detail)
Italian wool, hand-knitted to form 68 life-size snake replic
Largest: 59 1/2 x 3 in. (151.1 x 7.6 cm); smallest: 15 1/2 x 2 in. (39.1 x 5.1 cm)
Courtesy Dam, Stuhltrager Gallery, Brooklyn, New York

BELOW: *Coral Snake Series*, 2006 (detail)

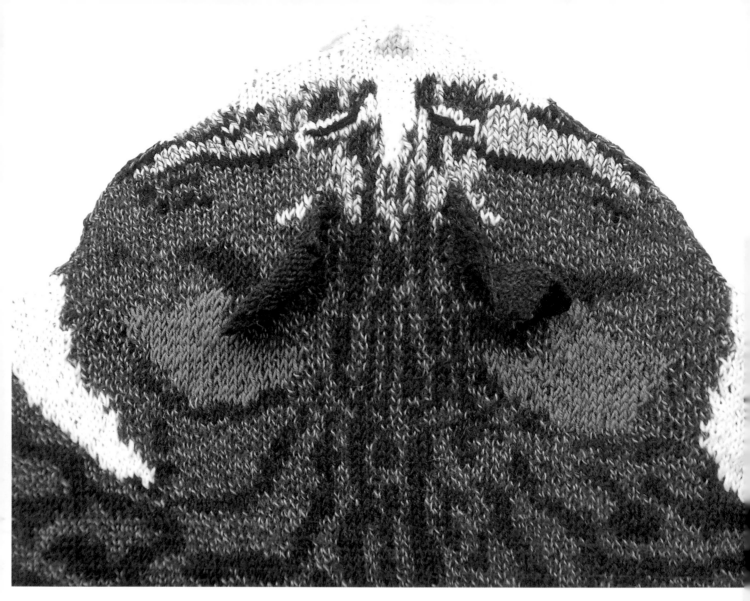

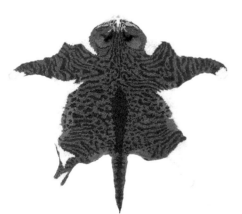

Rocky Rug, 2005 (detail above)
Hand-knitted wool yarn
39 x 45 x 1 ¹/₂ in.
(99.1 x 114.3 x 3.8 cm)
Collection of Brian Muller; courtesy Dam, Stuhltrager Gallery,
  Brooklyn, New York

Lacey Rocky, 2005
Yarn, t-pins, glass eyes
29 x 45 x 1 in. (73.7 x 114.3 x 2.5 cm)
Collection of Sharon Lombard Miller; courtesy Dam,
 Stuhltrager Gallery, Brooklyn, New York

matters of scale

Act Normal and That's Already Crazy Enough, 2003
Starched cotton fabric, computerized embroidery, copper
 wire, reed
19 in. x 9 ft. 4 in. x 11 ft. 8 in. (48.3 cm x 2.8 m x 3.6 m)
Collection of the artist

Act Normal and That's Already Crazy Enough, 2003 (detail)
Starched cotton fabric, computerized embroidery, copper
  wire, reed
19 in. x 9 ft. 4 in. x 11 ft. 8 in. (48.3 cm x 2.8 m x 3.6 m)
Collection of the artist

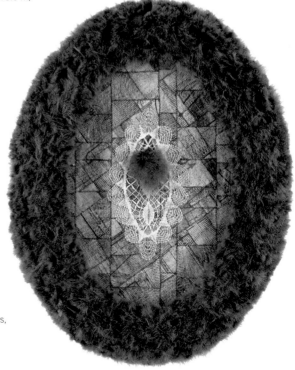

Family Air #4, 1998
Lace, contemporary Seminole patchwork, feathers,
  convex glass
27 x 21 x 2 in. (68.6 x 53.3 x 5.1 cm)
Collection of the artist

Echelman has reinvented public sculpture with her works, using fiber and the effects of wind currents to make large-scale pieces that are fluid and changing rather than fixed and imposing. Her application of lace knotting techniques to sculpture on a monumental scale thus subverts expectations of both the medium and its conventional forms.

Echelman began her artistic career as a painter. In 1997, only weeks away from an exhibition deadline while on a Fulbright Lectureship in India—and lacking paint supplies, which had been lost in transit—she took nightly walks along the beach, and had a revelation watching the fishermen pulling in their nets: "I was mesmerized by the form of their nets and the fact that they were so changeable and flexible. They became this three-dimensional form that had no weight." Forced to improvise, she enlisted the fishermen to help her use the netting to create several large-scale installations, which she called *Bellbottoms*.

That process became the template for her site-specific sculptures. For each work, Echelman researches the location (its environmental, cultural, and social aspects), then searches for experts who can help her in the creation of the piece—such as the grandmothers who showed her the lace techniques that she used for her installation at the Museum of the Centre of Europe in Vilnius, Lithuania, and the engineer (an expert in sails) who designed the proprietary software for modeling her nets according to different wind velocities and directions for her permanent installation of a 300-foot-diameter lace basket over a traffic circle in Porto, Portugal.

She Changes, 2005, the installation in Porto, is her largest to date. The Portuguese government commissioned Echelman to create a symbol for the city, to be located on its industrial waterfront, that would be visible from at least a kilometer in all directions, would not block any views of the ocean, and could survive high winds and salt air. The resulting sculpture consists of concentric circles of red-and-white netting made of Teflon fiber, hung from a 20-ton, steel-rimmed circle suspended by cables connected to three tall poles. The nets evoke fishing—historically, Porto's principal livelihood—while the colors recall the lighthouses dotting the coast and the area's modern industrial smokestacks.

As Echelman was sketching ideas for her work in this exhibition, *The Expanding Club*, 2007, designed for the Museum of Arts & Design stairwell atrium, the funnellike architectural space brought to mind a cloud; and with recent news reports of North Korea's testing of nuclear weapons, the cloud became a mushroom cloud. The colors she chose are the colors of the flags of all the countries that are known to have tested a nuclear bomb. The work, she notes, is a meditation on "the most violent weapon that we humans have ever created, using one of the oldest and most humble techniques of tying things together, repairing ourselves, and the world, one knot at a time."

—J.S.

b. 1966 in Tampa, Florida;
lives in New York and
in Brookline, Massachusetts
Education: B.A. (visual &
environmental studies), 1987,
Harvard University, Cambridge,
Massachusetts; M.F.A. (visual art)
1995, Milton Avery Graduate
School of the Arts, Bard College,
Annandale-on-Hudson, New York

ABOVE LEFT: Echelman standing underneath *Swooping II*, 2001, inside the Caja de Burgos, Spain, 2001

OPPOSITE: *Trying to Hide with Your Tail in the Air*, 1998
Hand-knotted nets, commercially manufactured nets, ste enamel, oak trees
35 x 9 x 9 ft. (10.7 x 2.7 x 2.7 m)
Museum of the Center of Europe, Vilnius, Lithuania
Courtesy Florence Lynch Gallery, New York

She Changes, 2005
Fiber, steel
H. 164 ft., Diam. 492 ft. (50 x 150 m)
Courtesy Florence Lynch Gallery, New York

She Changes, 2005 (aerial view)

She Changes, 2005 (evening view)

dave cole

b. 1975 in Etna, New Hampshire; lives in Providence, Rhode Island

Education: graduated 1992, Putney School, Putney, Vermont; graduated 1995, Landmark College, Putney; B.A. (visual arts), 1997, Brown University, Providence

While studying art at Brown University, Cole searched for ways to make his art accessible, not only to those familiar with conceptual art, but to anyone who had a genuine interest in it. "I was in school when the *Sensation* show opened [at the Brooklyn Museum of Art]; conceptually driven sculpture had gone beyond being esoteric and exclusive and into the realm of being intentionally offensive. One of the central challenges of making art is to engage the viewer; and when art is more and more abstract this becomes difficult. I get that, but I don't think the solution is to alienate and offend."

Cole found the solution he was looking for in knitting when, by chance, a teaching assistant in one of his studio classes challenged him to knit a sculpture. The resulting work, *Electric Blanket*, 1998, consists of contractor-grade electric cord that he arduously knit into a queen-size blanket, using two 4-foot-long needles. The experience convinced him that such a seemingly simple, accessible idea or pun, expressed through a traditional handcraft technique, could convey several layers of meaning.

Seeing the conceptual possibilities of the knitting process, and the kinds of forms that could be created, Cole began a series of explorations using various materials. For *Steel Wool Cap and Muffler*, 1998, he made a life-size hat and scarf using hand-spun steel-wool yarn. To do this, he constructed a spinning wheel utilizing technology illustrated in a nineteenth-century book on textile-mill management. "I figured out how the mechanism of a spinning wheel works from the engravings and re-created it in the studio." Surreal and visceral, the piece raised questions about production, industrial hazards, and ideas of comfort.

Later, Cole applied the knitting process to a larger-scale project, *Fiberglass Teddy Bear*, 2003: a gigantic teddy bear made of pink fiberglass construction insulation. This absurd and lovable stuffed toy swells into the surrounding space, simultaneously evoking feelings of comfort and danger. Cole used the same iconic image for a small-scale work he created for this exhibition: *Knit Lead Teddy Bear*, 2006, a 6-inch-high teddy bear made of lead ribbon; the toy is not only dangerous to touch, but difficult for a child to lift.

Also included in this exhibition is a new work by Cole, *Dollar Bill Dress*, based on a Vera Wang evening gown knitted from 879 $1 bills that he cut into "yarn" using a simple pair of scissors. The "yarn" was made by cutting each dollar bill to form a continuous narrow strip, beginning at one corner and cutting around and around toward the center. "The fact that I can take a dollar, destroy its integrity as a piece of paper, destroy its value as currency, inject a whole bunch of useless labor into it, and still end up with something that's worth $20,000 or more is amazing to me."

—J.S.E.

ABOVE LEFT: Dave Cole working on *Lead Teddy Bear* in his studio in Providence, 2004

OPPOSITE: *Fiberglass Teddy Bear*, 2003 (detail)
Fiberglass
14 x 14 x 14 ft. (4.3 x 4.3 x 4.3 m)
Courtesy Judi Rotenberg Gallery, Boston

BELOW: *Fiberglass Teddy Bear*, 2003

LEFT: *The Money Dress*, 2006
879 U.S. dollar bills, hand-cut to ⅛-inch width and knitted to "size 8"
70 x 24 x 18 in. (177.8 x 61 x 45.7 cm)
Courtesy Judi Rotenberg Gallery, Boston

BELOW: *Knit Lead Teddy Bear*, 2006
Lead ribbon, hand-cut and knitted over armature of lead wool
6 x 5½ x 4½ in. (15.2 x 14 x 11.4 cm)
Courtesy Judi Rotenberg Gallery, Boston

The Knitting Machine, 2005 (performance at MASS MoCA,
 North Adams, Massachusetts)
Acrylic felt, two John Deere excavators, telephone poles
Dimensions variable
Collection of the artist; courtesy Judi Rotenberg Gallery, Boston

althea merback

b. 1965 in Fort Collins, Colorado;

lives in Bloomington, Indiana

Education: B.S., 1988, School
of Allied Medicine, Ohio State
University, Columbus, Ohio

Merback was an avid knitter for many years before pursuing her fascination with miniatures. Ten years ago, while pregnant with triplets, she experienced a "flurry of activity," not only because she was required to rest, which gave her time to knit, but also because she had to make three of everything. Despite enjoying the meditative qualities of knitting, she found that she preferred its more mentally and physically engaging aspects. Moving beyond the search for difficult patterns, she set herself a challenge that involved enormous technical and creative hurdles.

Inspired by a miniature sweater offered on the Internet, Merback immediately scavenged her supplies for the thinnest yarn and the smallest needles she could find. She knitted her first miniature out of baby fingerling yarn, using size 0 needles. "At the time, I thought: 'Look at that—it's incredible!'" It was the smallest she had ever knit, but was extremely large and simply designed in comparison to what she would do next. Over a period of three years, Merback experimented with different materials to refine her process and perfect her scale to make truly minuscule garments.

To accurately knit at one-twelfth scale, Merback makes her own needles from stainless steel medical wire used for inserting I.V.'s. "I buy them in 60-inch lengths, cut them to my required length, then grind down and polish the ends to a dull point. The medical wire is perfect because it is straight and strong; and the needles are flexible, but never break." For her yarns, Merback uses fine threads in natural fibers such as cotton, wool, and silk from as far away as Australia and the Netherlands.

The creative foundation for the work is less technically driven. "When I have an idea, I like to do some research to inspire different possibilities." For her *Ancient Greek Pullover*, 2005, Merback studied the patterns, colors, motifs, functions, and symbolism of classical Grecian urns. The resulting design contains intricate intarsia patterns that form a vaselike silhouette, including a shaped neck, flared base, and arms that resemble handles. This is one example from an ongoing series of miniature garments with designs featuring art-historical themes (including ancient Egypt and twentieth-century Modernism), several of which are presented in this exhibition.

After determining the design and writing the pattern, it takes Merback more than five hundred hours to knit a single sweater. For her, the rewards of this labor-intensive process lie in overcoming limitations, defying conventions, and creating surprises: "I love the paradox of making something look exactly like something you could wear, but you can't because it's extremely tiny."

—J.S.E.

ABOVE LEFT: Merback using a magnifying glass to knit a miniature garment, Bloomington, Indiana, 2006

OPPOSITE: *Ancient Egyptian Cardigan*, 2005 (back)
Silk thread
2 1/4 x 1 1/4 in. (5.7 x 3.2 cm)
Kathleen Savage Browning Miniatures Collection, Kentuc
Gateway Museum Center, Maysville

BELOW: *Ancient Greek Gloves*, 2005
Silk thread
Each: 3/4 x 3/8 in. (1.9 x .9 cm)
Kathleen Savage Browning Miniatures Collection, Kentuc
Gateway Museum Center, Maysville

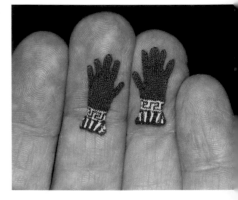

Picasso Cardigan, 2004 (front and back view)
Silk thread
2 1/2 x 1 3/4 in. (6.4 x 4.4 cm)
Kathleen Savage Browning Miniatures Collection, Kentucky
 Gateway Museum Center, Maysville

…nt Greek Pullover, 2005

…hread

…1 ¹/₂ in. (6.4 x 3.8 cm)

…een Savage Browning Miniatures Collection, Kentucky

…way Museum Center, Maysville

light
constructions

henk wolvers

b. 1953, Wageningen,
the Netherlands; lives in
's Hertogenbosch, the Netherlands
Education: 1974–79, Akademie
voor Beeldende Kunst/AKI,
Enschede, the Netherlands;
1977–78, Koninklijke Akademie
voor Kunst en Vormgeving,
's Hertogenbosch

Wolvers has devoted the past twenty years of his life to working exclusively with porcelain. He is fascinated by its translucency, which he exploits in subtle forms divorced from function. "I use the shape for a vase, bowl, or vessel, but I don't intend for it to hold fruit or liquid. It is more an object for decoration, not for use." Thus, Wolvers approaches each piece as sculpture—a vehicle with which to advance his understanding of the interplay of form, surface, and light.

Wolvers developed a process of applying color to paper-thin slabs of porcelain using stains (instead of more traditional glazes) to embed embellishments within the clay body, producing a variety of striking graphic patterns. This allows light to pass through and be captured within the walls of the form, closely linking the interior and exterior surfaces. Because of the thin walls of the porcelain and certain chemical properties of the oxide stains, the pigment and the clay combine during the firing in ways that create unpredictable movement: "Some stains have a higher melting point, and when I combine these with a white porcelain body there is movement in the kiln. I like that very much; it brings individuality to each piece that is important for me."

Wolvers began using reductive techniques to create lacelike openwork porcelain in 2002, puncturing and removing pieces from the slabs of clay before shaping them into vessels. He was intrigued by the increased transparency of form,

and the possibility of intensifying the visual connection between the interior and exterior surfaces. When he was invited to attend a three-month residency at the European Ceramic Work Center in the Netherlands in 2005, he saw it as an ideal opportunity to experiment further with porcelain lace-making techniques. "Porcelain is very difficult to work with. It is not possible to make all the forms you want with porcelain because there are certain restrictions imposed by the medium. It is nice to go beyond the edges of those limitations."

In creating a work for this exhibition, Wolvers used a strengthened porcelain slip and a painter's brush to slowly drip the fluid clay onto plaster kiln boards to form two large rectangular panels. When fired, the "drawings" shrank and hardened, creating a surface texture and composition of overlapping thick and thin lines that invite comparisons to Jackson Pollock's Abstract Expressionist "drip" paintings. The resulting porcelain lace panels are mounted a few inches away from the gallery walls, supported only by two wall-mounted nails, making them look as if they are suspended in space. The delicate openings invite a play of light, now more complex, which interlaces within, around, and through the porcelain, while elusive shadows cast on the walls surround and underscore the glowing form.

—J.S.E.

ABOVE LEFT: Wolvers opening the kiln in his studio in 's Hertogenbosch, 2006

OPPOSITE: *Lines I*, 2006
Porcelain
Each: 39 1/2 x 9 1/2 in. (100 x 24 cm)
Collection of the artist

BELOW: Material studies, 2006
Porcelain
Dimensions variable
Collection of the artist

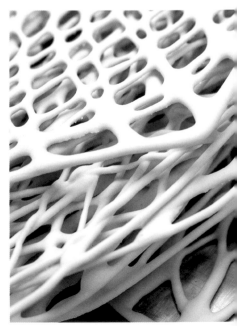

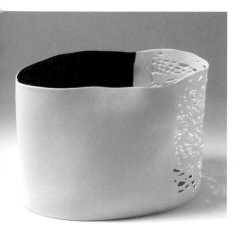

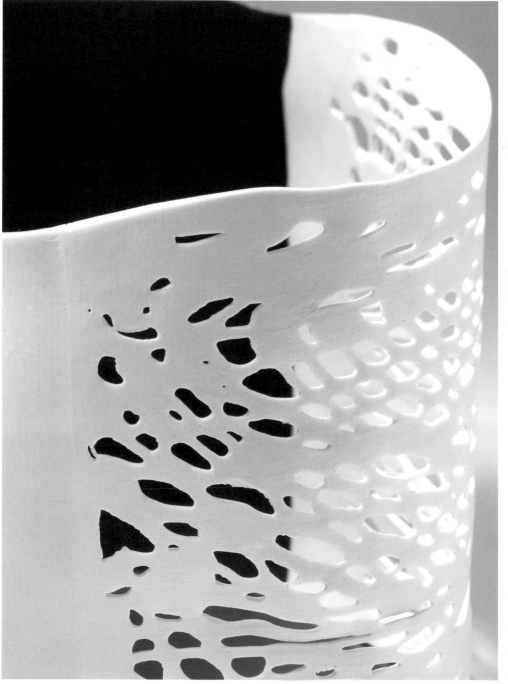

ABOVE: *Untitled*, 2006
porcelain, stain
8 x 9 x 6 in. (20 x 23 x 15 cm)
collection of the artist

RIGHT: *Untitled*, 2006 (detail)

OPPOSITE: *Lines II,* 2006 (detail)
porcelain, stain
39 in. x 23 ft. (100 cm x 7 m)
collection of the artist

niels van eijk

While studying at the Design Academy Eindhoven, van Eijk completed an apprenticeship at Gijs Bakker Design. He credits Bakker, co-founder of Droog Design, as being a primary influence on his own design philosophy. "Droog is what was taught at the academy; it was standard at the time." Droog focuses on the design of functional objects using conceptual ideas. Van Eijk made his *Cow Chair*, 1997, out of a single cowhide. "I wanted to make a chair out of leather, no more and no less. Finally I got there." It was accepted into the collection of Droog Design before he completed his studies at the academy that same year.

Van Eijk used a similar approach to create *Bobbin Lace Lamp*, 2002, his work presented in this exhibition. "I wanted to make a lamp without a bulb in it, and I wanted it to say something about light. Most lamps you see are some strange shape that doesn't have anything to do with the light itself." It took him three years to devise a solution to this problem, having discovered fiber optics early on in the design process, but only later finding the flexible type of fiber-optic cable that he would ultimately use in the finished piece. Its inherent properties led him to knot it into lace. "In this specific fiber-optic material, every fiber has 400 filaments in it. The fibers break at every knot, and that is how they lose light. I use the lace technique to break the fiber optics."

b.1970, Someren, the Netherlands; lives in Geldrop, the Netherlands

Education: Studied mechanical engineering, 1991, Polytechnic School, Helmond, the Netherlands; studied handicrafts, 1992, at TeHaTex, Nijmegan, the Netherlands; studied man and living, 1997, Design Academy Eindhoven, Eindhoven, the Netherlands

Van Eijk enlisted the help of an eighty-five-year-old neighbor who taught him traditional lace-making techniques. "It is very important to work with the people who actually do it. It doesn't have to be craftsman; it could be welders, or laser cutters. They can teach me about the techniques and ways to get a step further." This exposure to actual lace making and old pattern books from the library gave him the foundation required to develop his ideas into a finished product. The interwoven wires form the structure of the lamp's upper half (the "lampshade") and end as fringe in the lamp's lower half. Rather than being simply a decorative addition, the wires are both the natural extension of the structure and (at their ends) the functional transmitters of light.

—J.S.E.

ABOVE LEFT: Van Eijk working on his *Bobbin Lace Lamp*, Someren, 2006

OPPOSITE: *Bobbin Lace Lamp*, 2002
Fiber optics, metal wire
H. 9 ft. 10 in., Diam. 31 1/2 in. (300 cm x 80 cm)
Museum Boymans van Beuningen, Rotterdam, the Netherlands; Dutch Textile Museum, Tilburg, the Netherlands; Manchester City Art Gallery, Manchester England

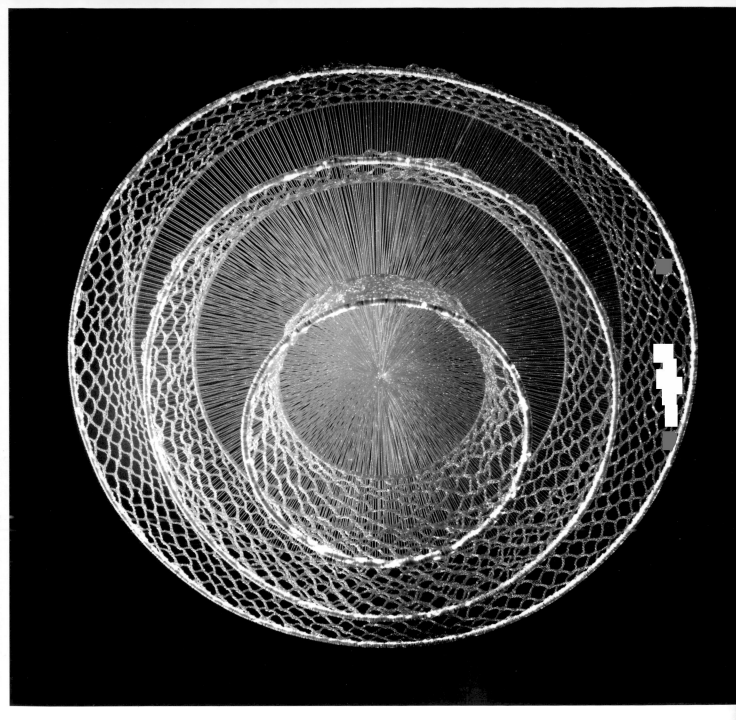

Bobbin Lace Lamp, Vegas, 2005
Fiber optics
H. 6 ft. 6 3/4 in., Diam. 8 ft. 2 1/2 in. (2 x 2.5 m)
Le Rêve (beauty salon), Las Vegas, Nevada

OPPOSITE: *Bobbin Lace Lamp*, 2002 (detail)

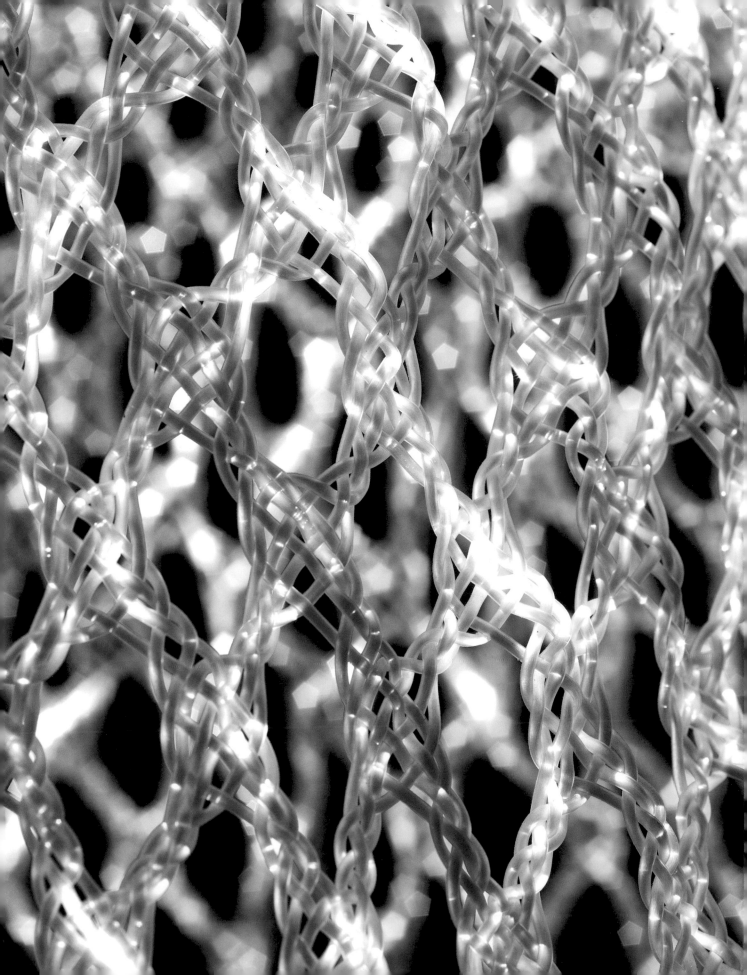

bennett battaile

b. 1960 in Woodland, California; lives in Portland, Oregon

Education: B.A. (mathematics), 1982, St. Olaf College, Northfield, Minnesota; M.S. (computer science), 1985, Cornell University, Ithaca, New York

Battaile applies mathematical concepts to structural form to make lacelike glass sculptures. These complex lattices composed of thin glass rods are visualizations of math problems that interest him. As he explains, "I find a visual idea in math, I see if I can picture it, and then I try to bring in multiple ideas and mix them together. Eventually I will come up with an idea which I can't picture, which makes it interesting, and I try to make a sculpture of it."

Battaile's work in glass was initially inspired by mathematical problems that needed to be graphed in three dimensions, which led him to search for ways to create a "three-dimensional blackboard." He thought he had found a solution when he came across the glass technique of flameworking (heating thin rods of glass with a small, concentrated flame to bend them and attach them to each other). In 1996, he took a flameworking class from artist Anna Skibska at the Pilchuck Glass School in Seattle. Although he discovered that the process was too slow for graphing purposes, he was fascinated by the technique and the material, and continued to explore its artistic (and mathematical) potential.

Flameworking allows Battaile to construct his pieces a single element at a time, essentially sketching in glass. Battaile notes that while there are some similarities between flameworked glass and fiber—the rods have a certain amount of give, and can be wrapped or looped around each other to form a "woven" structure—he creates the basic structure of each sculpture through connections and bracing pieces, rather than knots or loops. The link with lace remains visual and conceptual.

The initial inspiration for *History*, 2005, Battaile's piece in this exhibition, was a gyroid shape, composed of a series of connected saddle-shaped curves, which he set out to make using a formula known as a Hilbert space-filling curve—a line that is continually doubled back on itself by bending it again and again until it fills up an entire space. Here, the line formed by the black glass fills up the entire surface of the gyroid. Theoretically, if the two ends of this line were grasped and the line stretched out, one would see that it was continuous and does not knot or loop over itself. The clear glass serves as structural support. Even without any knowledge of the particular underlying mathematical concepts, viewers can appreciate the elegant structure as it interacts with light.

—J.S.

ABOVE LEFT: Bennett Battaile in his studio in Portland, 200(

OPPOSITE: *History*, 2005
Clear and black flameworked glass
37 x 36 x 36 in. (94 x 91.4 x 91.4 cm)
Collection of the artist

BELOW: Gyroid image from Eric W. Weisstein, "Gyroid," from MathWorld–A Wolfram Web Resource, *http://mathw wolfram.com/Gyroid.html*

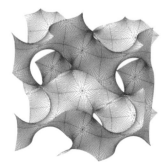

Déjà Vu, 2003
Flameworked glass
13 x 13 x 13 in. (33 x 33 x 33 cm)
Private collection

OPPOSITE: *Mirage for Susan*, 2006 (detail)
Clear and black flameworked glass
13 x 14 x 7 in. (33 x 35.6 x 17.8 cm)
Collection of Susan Thayer

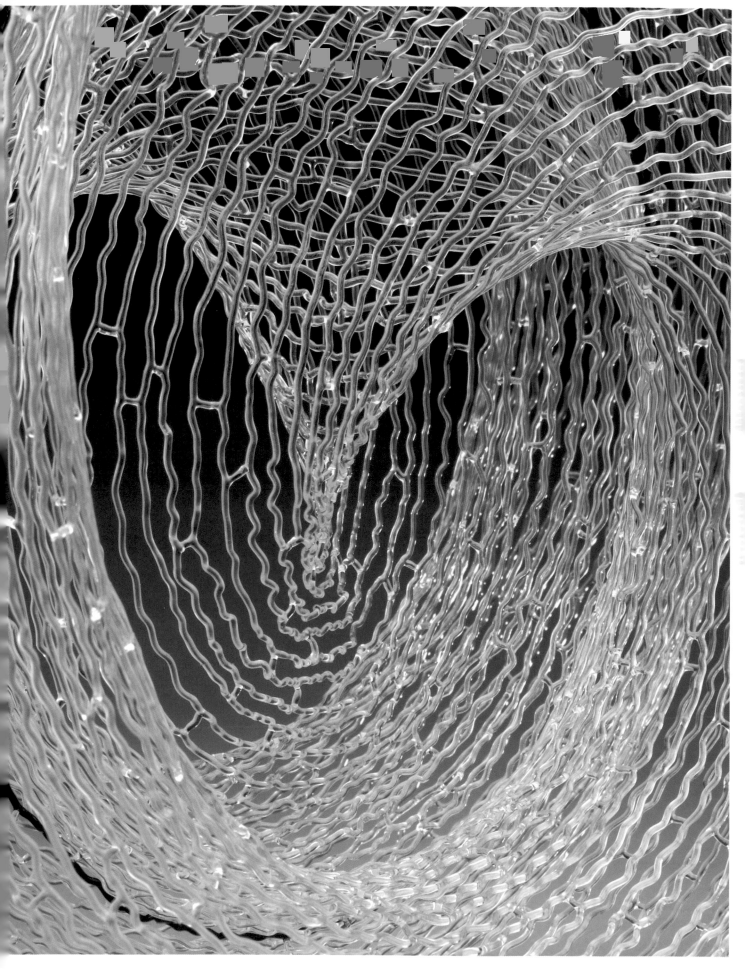

interconnections

b. 1977 in Washington D.C.;

lives in New York

Education: B.A. (art/semiotics),
2000, Brown University,
Providence, Rhode Island

In her multifaceted art practice, Gschwandtner defies categorization. As a filmmaker, she frequently produces works that relate some aspect of knitting or textiles—tactility, hand process, textile skills—to filmmaking. As a curator, she organizes art events that incorporate participatory knitting sessions, knit artwork, and knitting-related performances or installations. And as the founding editor of the magazine *KnitKnit*, she seeks to identify and develop a community of people who use knitting as a creative outlet in various ways, and to disseminate information about these people and their work to the general public in a format that is in itself a work of art.

Films shown in movie theaters tend to negate the physical existence of the roll of film: the projection room is hidden from the audience, and the filmmaker tries to make the audience forget about the projection space and enter the reality of the projected image. Gschwandtner instead emphasizes the materiality of the film. For her work *Crochet Film*, 2004, a site-specific installation, the duration of the film clip was limited to the length of the space of the installation. The viewer was obliged to walk next to the 80-foot film loop down the length of the installation in order to see the projected image at the end of a corridor, and thus was fully aware of the physicality of the film, its movement, and the composition of frames that, shown rapidly in succession, created the illusion of movement. The action depicted on film was Gschwandtner crocheting a replica of the film loop in yarn (further emphasizing the materiality of the film); and the wool replica was turning on a metal spool positioned alongside the loop of film that—while turning on its metal spool—was being projected.

KnitKnit magazine explores the intersection of craft and contemporary art in articles, reviews, interviews, and photographic essays. In addition, each issue has been produced with a special handmade cover, and is accompanied by art events that become participatory exhibitions. For example, the *KnitKnit Sundown Salon*, held in 2004 in a geodesic dome in Los Angeles, included exhibitions, performances, screenings, and participatory activities.

The work that Gschwandtner has created for this exhibition is an interactive project—a book that will be assembled during the show's run at the Museum, incorporating materials made by visitors who take part in a "knitting circle" while they are here, using patterns based on photographs of knitting in wartime (on display nearby) —along with documentation of the project. Consistent with her art practice, this ambitious work explores intersections among different mediums and forms of expression to focus attention on the artistic, social, and historical contexts of knitting.

—J.S.

ABOVE LEFT: Gschwandtner in her studio in New York, 2

OPPOSITE: Josh Faught
Hand-crocheted cover of *KnitKnit*, issue no. 5, 2005,
using yarn by Ozark Handspun
9 x 6 in. (20.3 x 15.2 cm)
St. Lawrence University, Canton, New York

BELOW: Sabrina Gschwandtner
Hand-made covers of *KnitKnit*, issue no. 1, 2002
Spray-printed fabric
Each, 8 1/2 x 6 1/2 in. (21.6 x 16.5 cm)
The Museum of Modern Art/Franklin Furnace Artist's
Book Collection, New York

het Film, 2004 (installation view at Sculpture Center,
g Island City, New York)
projector, 80-ft. loop of 16mm film, 80-ft. loop of
cheted wool yarn
nsions variable
ction of the artist
e: both objects were labeled with their length and
ion: Film (80 ft., 2:14 min); Film Replica (80ft., 575
The film depicts the artist crocheting the yarn loop.]

still from *The KnitKnit Sundown Salon,* 2004
:o, 6 mins. 36 secs.)
n National Academy of the Arts, Norway

TE: Liz Collins
ne-knitted cover of *KnitKnit*, issue no. 4, 2004
า. (20.3 x 15.2 cm)
ion of Sabrina Gschwandtner

cat mazza

Mazza's art practice combines anti-sweatshop activism, technology, and handcrafts, highlighting the connections among all three. Mazza began knitting while working with computers in electronic media arts, as a way to relax as well as to reconnect with more physical, tactile activity. As her interest in knitting grew, she began to notice certain similarities with her work in computer programming. The digital imaging that she was doing on a Web site—manipulating a series of pixels on a grid screen—was similar to composing textile patterns based on the grid. This parallel led her to create her knitPro computer program. Available for free on Mazza's Web site (www.microRevolt.org), the program allows anyone to upload any images they have access to and transforms them into knitting, crochet, needlepoint, or cross-stitch patterns "on a grid sizable for any fiber project."

The knitPro program also became a tool used in Mazza's political activism around issues of sweatshop labor used by major clothing manufacturers. These ubiquitous symbols of mass production and consumption are the basis of knitted projects that generate questions such as "What does this symbol mean?," "Why is it glorified in our culture?," and "Who is creating the stitchwork behind the product that we buy off the shelf?"

b. 1977 in Washington, D.C.;
lives in Troy, New York
Education: B.F.A. (studio art),
1999, Carnegie Mellon University,
Pittsburgh, Pennsylvania; M.F.A.
(integrated electronic arts),
2005, Rensselaer Polytechnic
Institute, Troy, New York

In 2003, Mazza began her *Nike Blanket Petition* to raise awareness about sweatshop conditions. "The idea was to start a handmade collaborative petition. Instead of a traditional activists' incentive where you sign a petition, I liked this idea of having people handmake a petition by knitting or crocheting one." The handmade petition emphasized the ways in which mass-produced garments are made, and underscored the amount of work that goes into making them. In addition to incorporating square knitted panels sent to her by petitioners, Mazza also made the petition available on her Web site, where participants could sign online and a knitted square would be added to the blanket for them. The signers' names show up on their square on the Web site, combining the virtual component with the actual physical blanket. The project continues to grow, as squares for the blanket's border are sent from all over the world.

Mazza's latest project is *Knitoscope*, a computer-animation program that translates her hand-knitted panels into moving images. Using this program, she creates videos that look as if they were film animations of her knitted images, even though they are computer-generated. The videos focus on the labor movement, continuing Mazza's involvement with these issues.

—J.S.

ABOVE LEFT: Mazza in her studio with Arthur Jones, Rensselaer Polytechnic Institute, Troy, New York, 2005

OPPOSITE, CLOCKWISE FROM UPPER LEFT: *Knitoscope Scre* *Shot III*, 2006
Knitoscope animation software with digital-video feed

Knitoscope Screen Shot I, 2006
Knitoscope animation software with digital-video feed

Knitoscope Screen Shot II, 2006
Knitoscope animation software with digital-video feed

Knitoscope Screen Shot IV, 2006
Knitoscope animation software with digital-video feed

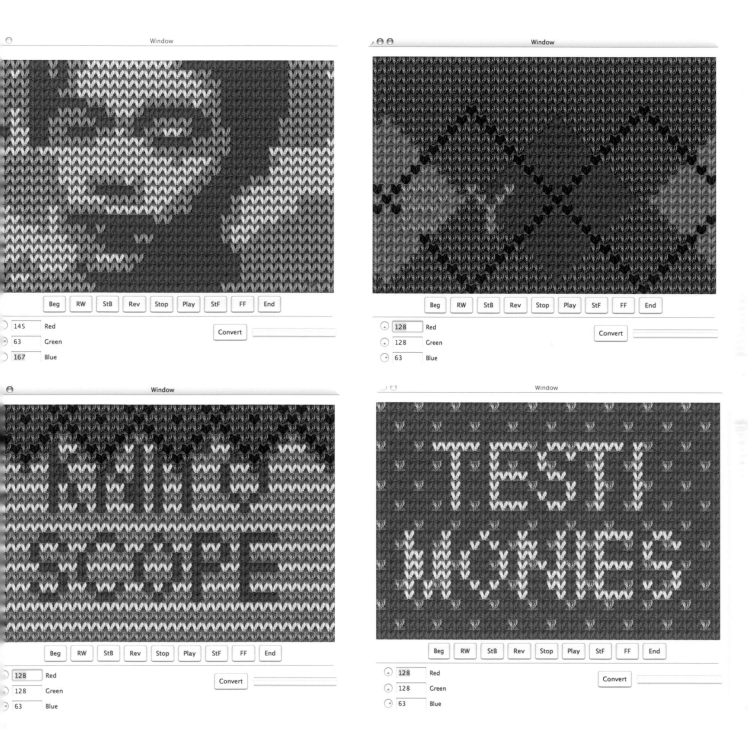

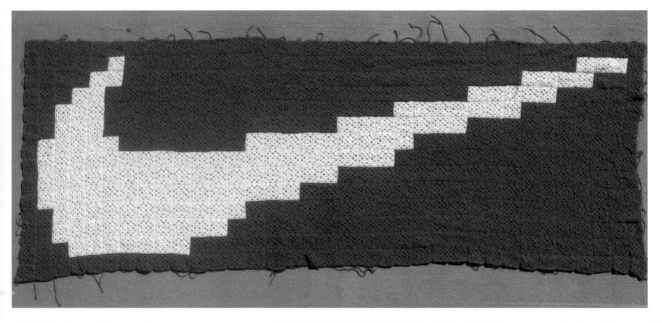

ABOVE: *Nike Blanket Petition,* (work in progress)
Crocheted wool
56 in. x 11 ft. 8 in. (142.2 cm x 3.6 m)
Collection of the artist

LEFT: *Mickey Face Mask Logoknit*, 2004 (modeled at
  Tactical Media Lab, Troy, New York)
Wool knitted using knitPro pattern

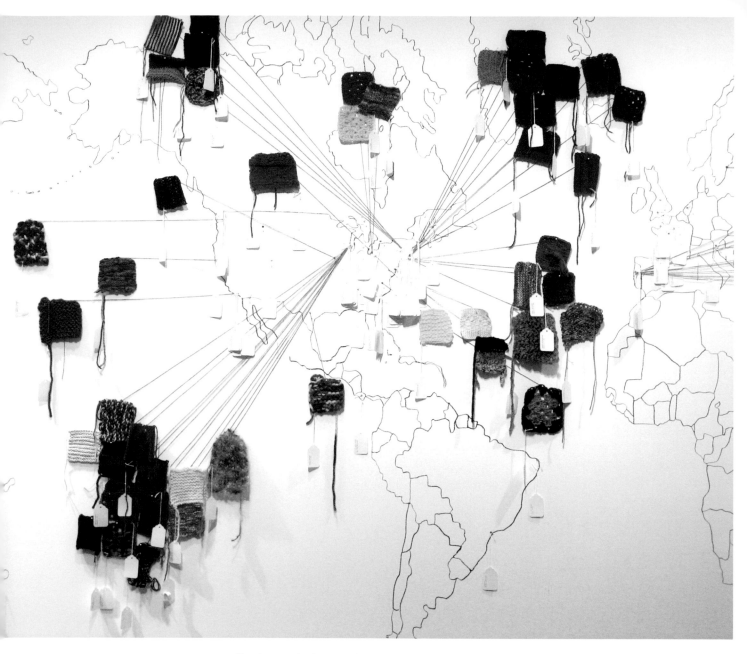

Map documenting the origin of petition squares for the border of the *Nike Blanket Petition*.

françoise dupré

b. 1953 in Paris; lives in London

Education: B.A. (sculpture), 1982, Camberwell School of Art, London; M.A. (history and theory of modern art), Chelsea School of Art and Design, London

For Dupré, knitting is both a process and a symbol, an opportunity for individual creative expression and for collaborative transcultural exchange. In her installations and her community-based work alike, she uses French spool knitting. She chose this technique for its simplicity and its versatility, since it can be easily taught to non-knitters, and can be done with many different materials and produce works of varied scale.

Dupré bases much of her work on art-historical and social theory. Her studies in feminist theory have led her to explore techniques and mediums that have been traditionally associated with women, and consequently undervalued. She is also influenced by philosopher Michel de Certeau's writings on the creation of "everyday" artwork by people not involved in "high" culture, who instead use materials they have at hand, and she frequently incorporates recycled and found objects into her works. Inspired by anthropologist Fernando Ortiz's concepts of the transcultural, and of creativity as an expression of the individual's rebellion against globalization, Dupré organizes projects that empower marginalized segments of society and facilitate cultural exchange.

For many of her projects, she collaborates with a group of people in a specific location, and attempts to bring in as many elements of the local culture and geography as she can. For a residency at the Irish Museum of Modern Art in Dublin, she worked with a group of Irish knitters.

The finished installation work, *snáth nasc, de fil en aiguille*, 2004, incorporated references to the garden that surrounded the museum, as well as stitches that were particular to Irish knitting, and a thin strip of images around the installation site, culled from a video that documented the project. The knitters participated in every stage of the project, from conception to installation.

Dupré's work with a group of Somali women at the UK Crafts Council in London became a source of community for immigrant women who had left everything behind. The project evolved through group discussion and experimentation, rather than according to a plan established by the artist. At the finish, the resulting object reminded the Somali women of a stack of baskets called a *fujaan*, given by the bride's family to the groom's family during a traditional Somali wedding.

Dupré's piece for this exhibition, *Fleur Bleue (Blue Flower)*, 2007, is made out of the blue bottle caps of a brand of French mineral water, and connected with black elastic; it refers to an old-fashioned French textile print that her grandmother used to wear. *Fleur bleue* is also a French term that describes someone (generally a woman) or something (like a dress or a novel) that is sentimental or old-fashioned. This work emphasizes one of the most important themes in Dupré's work: the celebration of the beauty found in everyday life.

—J.S.

ABOVE LEFT: Dupré in a performance work making *French Knitting with Rubber*, part of *La Résidente*, an installation the Irish Museum of Modern Art, Dublin, 2003

OPPOSITE: *Fleur Bleue*, 2007 (detail)

BELOW: *Fleur Bleue*, 2007 (detail)
Nylon, elastic, woven Hi-Py, glass, mirrored glass, acrylic, pins, plastic bottle tops
8 ft. x 8 ft. x 1 in. (2.5 m x 2.5 m x 3 cm)
Collection of the artist

French Knitting, 2003 (installation view at The Gallery,
Stratford-upon-Avon, England, 2003)
Wool, mirrors, hat pins, lenses, feather, Lycra, hair clips,
glitter
42 in. x 23 ft. x 1 1/2 in. (106.7 cm x 7 m x 3.8 cm)
Collection of the artist

RIGHT: *Fujaan*, 2005 (community-based project at the
Craft Council, London, for the exhibition *Knit 2 Together:
New Concepts in Knitting*)
Synthetic yarn, wire, sequins
6 ½ ft. x 15 ½ in. x 15 ½ in. (2 m x 40 cm x 40 cm)
Created in collaboration with the Somali women's group,
Back to Basics, and its group leader, Rakhia Ismail

3 video stills from *Here and There,
French Knitting, Brixton,* 2003
(video, 27 mins.)
Collection of the artist

shane waltener

b. 1966 in Brussels, Belgium;
lives in London

Education: B.A. (fine arts),
1989, Camberwell College of
Art and Craft, London; M.A.
(sculpture), 1991, Chelsea College
of Arts, London; Post-diploma,
1992, École des Beaux-Arts,
Marseille, France

Waltener's knitted works are intended as interruptions: interruptions in physical space, but also interruptions in time, offering some brief respite from the frenetic pace and consumerism of modern life. His installations and his collaborative performance pieces (in which he encourages public participation) propose needlecraft as a more thoughtful way of creating art, emphasizing human connections and interactions.

Waltener's collaborative work began with the London group Cast Off, founded by knitters Rachael Matthews and Amy Plant in 2000. Inviting participation in lively social events that reframed knitting as young, dynamic, and anti-establishment, Cast Off staged "knit-ins" on London subways, at the Savoy Hotel bar (a group of about 30 in 2003), and at the Victoria and Albert Museum (a crowd of more than 4,000 in 2004). Waltener has continued the practice of participatory knitting circles on his own at various venues, including the Prague biennale, in which a small group sits in a circle, sharing circular needles and knitting in one big multicolored loop. These works become part performance art, part community building: "People just drop in. They participate and share their thoughts and experiences about knitting, and then we'll talk about art, so it's about focusing on the here and now."

Waltener's installations often incorporate crocheted lace, presenting themes of connection and communication in purely visual terms. *Aunt Peggie Has Departed*, 2003, installed in an abandoned London subway station that was used as a bomb shelter during World War II, combined visual and aural elements. Waltener hung crocheted "cobwebs" there inside a series of 1940s phone booths, and incorporated a soundtrack that included Churchill's voice and period radio clips, thereby evoking the past and suggesting the "webs" of communication created through telephone conversations. The patterns he used for the cobwebs were part of the legacy of the real Aunt Peggy, who left needlecraft patterns to Waltener when she died. Another of his crocheted lace installation pieces, *The 26,000*, at the deconsecrated church of St. Mary at Lambeth (now London's Museum of Garden History), features 26,000 knots, referring to the 26,000 people buried there. The time and patience required to make this work seem an appropriate homage to the paupers and prostitutes buried in the churchyard.

Other crocheted installations are deliberate disruptions of a site. *Chihuly Doily #1* was a giant cobweb of elastic enclosing a Dale Chihuly chandelier, installed in the grand lobby of the Victoria and Albert Museum (in conjunction with the Cast Off knit-in there in 2004), mocking the formal grandeur of its neoclassical architecture and its stature as a cultural arbiter. Waltener's webs—witty decorative elements in an austere architectural space, and signifiers of neglect in an institution devoted to conservation—undermine such authority. *A World Wide Web*, 2007, Waltener's installation for the current exhibition at the Museum, similarly disrupts the gallery space. The knitted "cobwebs" that stretch across the galleries impede the path of viewers, while the lace eyelets serve as peepholes that provide a constantly shifting outlook as they walk on through. Using such strategies, Waltener forces both a literal and a figurative change of perspective.

—J.S.

ABOVE LEFT: Waltener during a performance at South Hill Park, Bracknell, England, 2006

OPPOSITE: *Chihuly Doily #1*, 2004 (detail)

BELOW: *Chihuly Doily #1*, 2004 (installation view at Victor and Albert Museum, London)
Shirring elastic, extant Dale Chihuly glass chandelier
Approx. 10 x 13 x 13 ft. (3 x 4 x 4 m)
Collection of the artist

Auntie Peggy Has Departed, 2003
(installation views at an extant abandoned Underground Station, London)
Mercerized cotton, telephone booths, 2-track audio loop,
audio equipment
10 x 39 1/2 x 6 1/2 ft. (3 x 12 x 2 m)
Collection of the artist

ABOVE LEFT: *Knitting Piece #11* (Prague), 2005 (performance
 at *nEUclear Reaction* exhibition, National Gallery, Prague
 Biennial, Prague)
Wool, circular needles, chairs, people knitting
Dimensions variable
Courtesy MKgalerie.nl

BELOW LEFT AND ABOVE: *Knitting Piece #5* (Berlin), 2004
 (performance at *ArtForum Berlin 2004,* Berlin)
Wool, circular needles, chairs, people knitting
Dimensions variable
Courtesy MKgalerie.nl

creative
deconstructions

cal lane

For Lane, art has been one of the few constants in a life of frequently changing careers and extreme life experience. "I don't think I was unsettled, I just wanted to try and taste everything. I still approach life the same way; I see making art as a way of combining the world in my head together with the world outside." In her work, Lane uses popular associations of lace as a means of expressing life's inherent contradictions: lace can conceal and reveal, convey comfort and lust, and is often used in rituals as divergent as weddings and funerals.

"When I was working as a welder, I found myself tidying up the metal shop, and suddenly felt conscious of being female. As a joke for the men who worked in the morning, I placed doilies on the machinery—on the band saw, anvil, drill press. It was a kind of marking of territory, I think, and visually, I liked how this clean, white, delicate object draped over the dirty, oily, steel machine, protected it." Later, Lane decided to make her own doily out of the industrial steel that she had learned to cut and manipulate with a welding torch, as a way of commenting on notions of femininity and cleanliness.

Consistent with her interest in contrasts, Lane's lace making involves two entirely different processes. Her first explorations in lace making involved a reductive process that she likens to both drawing and sculpture: "Cutting with an oxyacetylene torch functions as both a drawing instrument and a carving instrument; it is very manual. Slag is produced, and an uneven rough line is made, becoming evidence of the hand-made, as in a lace doily or a drawing, but in a hard, cold, heavy-duty, structural steel plate. It brings about a kind of balance as well as humor to an object."

The other process is one she adopted from her grandmother: "I used to watch her decorate cupcakes by placing a doily on top of the cake, sifting icing sugar through it, and removing the doily to expose a powdered print." Lane adapted this domestic technique to her industrial form of art by sifting soil through large pieces of lace, covering, coating and burying objects and people. "It creates a dialogue of beautiful filth. On the people, it is dirty, sexy, beautiful and morbid. On the floor, it relates to ornamental rugs, a temporary form of printmaking to be later swept up."

Lane has used several of these ideas and techniques in her installation for this exhibition. Objects once relied on for their durability, strength, and function now exist as delicate, decorative skeletons. The applied dirt and flaking rust offer an ephemeral layer to the sturdy and still placement of form, becoming "a kind of residue of the objects themselves, like a trace of what was once there, but fragile."

—J.S.E.

b. 1968 in Halifax, Nova Scotia, Canada; lives in Putnam Valley, New York

Education: Graduated 1993 (fine arts diploma), Victoria College of Art, Victoria, Canada; studied welding, 1996, Camosun College, Victoria, Canada; B.F.A., 2001, Nova Scotia College of Art and Design, Nova Scotia, Canada; M.F.A., 2001, Purchase College, State University of New York, Purchase, New York

ABOVE LEFT: Lane working in her studio in Peekskill, New York, 2006

OPPOSITE: *Untitled*, 2006 (installation views at Scope Art New York)
Dimensions variable
Plasma-cut wheelbarrow and shovels, flame-cut steel I-beams, soil, tomato paste
Courtesy Foley Gallery, New York

5 Shovels, 2005
Plasma-cut shovels
Each shovel, 57 x 8 x 8 in. (144.8 x 20.3 x 20.3 cm)
Collection of Robert and Tracey Hain; courtesy Foley Gallery,
 New York

OPPOSITE: *Fabricate*, 2002 (detail, installation view at
 Art Gallery of Nova Scotia)
Flame-cut steel I-beams
Dimensions variable
Courtesy Foley Gallery, New York

b. 1962, Willimantic, Connecticut;

lives in Baltimore, Maryland

Education: B.F.A (fiber), 1985,
Philadelphia College of Art,
Philadelphia; M.F.A (fiber), 1988,
Cranbrook Academy of Art,
Bloomfield Hills, Michigan

Shepard began thinking about the connections between fiber and architecture as an under-graduate, and was later influenced by Anni Albers's essay "The Pliable Plane: Textiles in Architecture." Although the two seem inherently different—architecture as solid, rigid, fixed; fiber as pliable, transportable—they often serve the same function of protecting, sheltering, serving as a point of separation between the outside world and the body. Her work explores this dichotomy by using fabric to create architectural installations that question our notions of strength, solidity, and fragility.

In the 1990s, Shepard began making pierced fabric, working with an acid-etching technique called devoré. From there, she moved on to cutting the fabric, which became a way for her to explore the nature of her material: "I am interested in the materiality of cloth, the physical tolerances of the material, in thinking about this cloth as a kind of membrane or skin, and the idea that the cutting of it pushes it toward its most fragile limit."

Shepard adds further layers of meaning to her works by incorporating references to historical patterns. After a sabbatical in India during which she became interested in *Jali* screens, she created *Screen*, 2001; and she made *Chambers*, 2002, after researching early-twentieth-century textile patterns. She started using lace patterns for historical reference when the Baltimore Museum of Art asked her to create a work based on their Cone collection of historical laces. The resulting series of installations, entitled *Filigree Spaces*, was presented at the museum in 2005, along with an exhibition of historical laces. Although Shepard does not use lace techniques in creating her works, she has studied lace making. To her, the labor-intensive cutting process that she employs is a reference to and reflection of the time and skill that goes into the creation of traditional lace. "Particularly with lace," she observes, "I can't help but marvel at its technology and its complexity. In that sense, lace is an acknowledgement of my history and my medium, and I am reflecting on that tradition and drawing connections to it."

Lace Meander, 2007, the piece that she made for this exhibition, consists of a long, 8-foot-wide piece of cloth with two narrower borders, all pierced with a historical lace pattern and hanging from ceiling to floor on industrial spools. The delicacy and fragility of the lace patterns contrast with the heavy metal spools and the large scale of the installation. The spools seem to suggest mechanical production, while the cloth makes obvious reference to meticulous hand labor; and what may be deemed ornamental becomes architectural.

—J.S.

ABOVE LEFT: Shepard in her studio in Baltimore, 2005

OPPOSITE: *Lace Meander*, 2006 (detail)
Muslin, gesso, graphite, aluminum
Dimensions variable
Collection of the artist

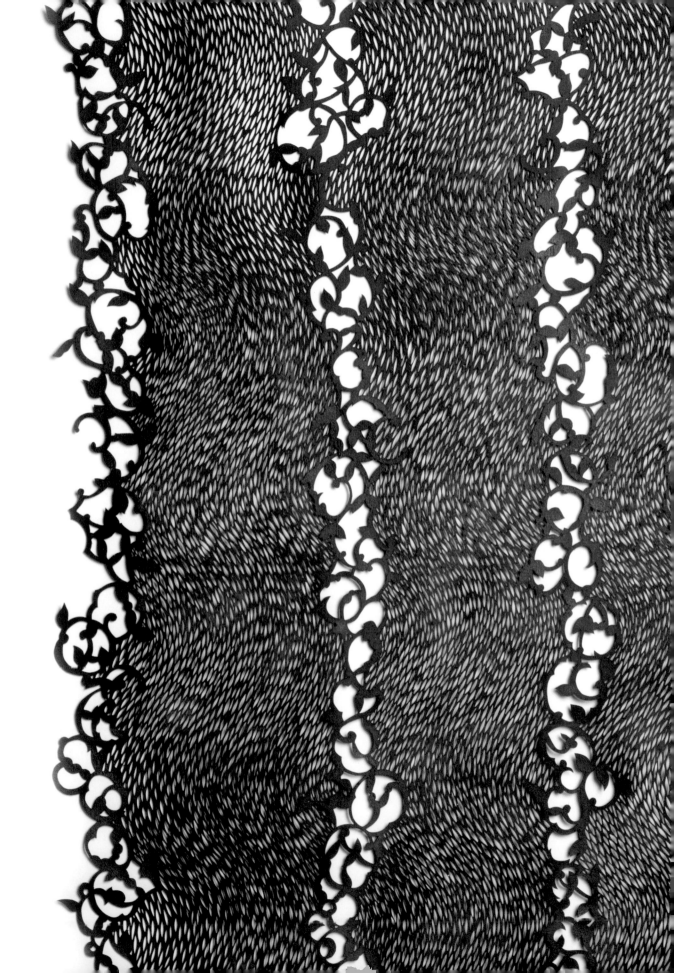

Along Lace Lines, 2005 (detail)
Hand-cut muslin, gesso, graphite, brass and aluminum
 armature
15 ft. x 36 ft. x 6 in. (4.6 m x 11.1 m x 15.2 cm)
Baltimore Museum of Art; Lilian Sarah Greif Bequest Fur
 BMA 2005.63.1–9

W: *Chambers*, 2002 (installation view at Baltimore
eum of Art, 2005)
-cut muslin, ink, gesso, steel armatures
els each 9 ft. x 47 in. x 18 in.
m x 119.4 cm x 45.7 cm)
ction of the artist

overing, 2005 (installation view at Baltimore
eum of Art, 2005)
printed devoré cloth, wood
nsions variable
ction of the artist

: Chambers, 2002 (detail)

elana herzog

b. 1954 in Toronto, Canada;
lives in New York

Education: M.F.A. (sculpture), 1979, State University of New York, Alfred, New York; B.A., 1976, Bennington College, Bennington, Vermont

Historically, hand-made lace was the product of a rigid, structured, and exacting process; quality was measured by the complexity of pattern and the resulting invisibility of hand. Herzog's relief sculptures—haunting, abstract, lacelike wall panels—retain the complex and laborious nature of the lace-making process and convey ideas of material culture, domestic nostalgia, time, and decay.

For each sculpture, Herzog deconstructs a found carpet or chenille bedspread to create a unique lacelike remnant. For *Untitled*, 2004, from the installation *Civilization and Its Discontents*, 2005, which is presented in this exhibition, she chose as her material a Persian carpet that was once in the living room of her childhood home. "It is something I stared at so many times, and although it eventually had been worn almost beyond recognition, I still knew it really intimately; it was embedded in my visual repertoire." Using the worn and partly eroded fabric as a starting point, she created an entirely new composition by a process of removing and adding threads and tufts.

The process is an organic one. She begins by attaching the woven fabric to the wall with hundreds of staples, following an existing pattern or weave structure. The applied staples puncture and pinch the material, pinning and compressing the aged, worn textile to the wall. "I then pick away at the fibers and pry staples from the wall until, eventually, in certain areas of the piece, all that remain are the perforations on the wall, an abraded surface whose remnants of a pattern suggests something lacelike."

Simultaneously digging into the surface in some areas, and building it up in others by reapplying what has been torn away, Herzog systematically reworks the piece until the textures on the wall are seamlessly integrated with the fiber remnants, thus activating the architecture and creating an ambiguity between figure and ground. "Lace allows for that possibility because you get areas that are very open and other areas that are very dense. There is this fluidity between what you see through it and what you see around it."

In *Untitled*, 2005, a site-specific installation that she made at the Sculpture Center in Long Island City in 2005, Herzog integrated the architecture even further by building walls that wrap around and encircle the viewer. The weathered surface on the existing gallery walls echoed the aggressive deconstruction of the fabric panels to create a visual contrast with the newly constructed, crisp white walls. "I loved being able to make a transition between their walls, which are so rich and evocative, to my walls, which had a different reference but somehow seemed compatible." By methodically and forcefully working the textile into the architecture, Herzog created torn and perforated patterns to form a lacelike surface partly muddied by the laborious and often violent actions that created it.

—J.S.E.

ABOVE LEFT: Herzog in her studio in Walton, New York, 2(

OPPOSITE: *Untitled*, 2004, from the installation *Civilization and Its Discontents*, 2005
Wool carpet, miscellaneous fabrics, staples in gypsum or plywood panel
78 x 67 in. (198 x 170 cm)
Collection of the artist

BELOW: *So Bennington*, 2005 (installation view, Usdan Ga Bennington College, Bennington, Vermont)
Bedspread, staples in gypsum on plywood panel
Dimensions variable
Collection of the artist

Untitled, 2005 (installation view at the Sculpture Center,
 Long Island City, New York)
Polyester chenille bedspreads, staples in gypsum on
 plywood panel
Dimensions variable

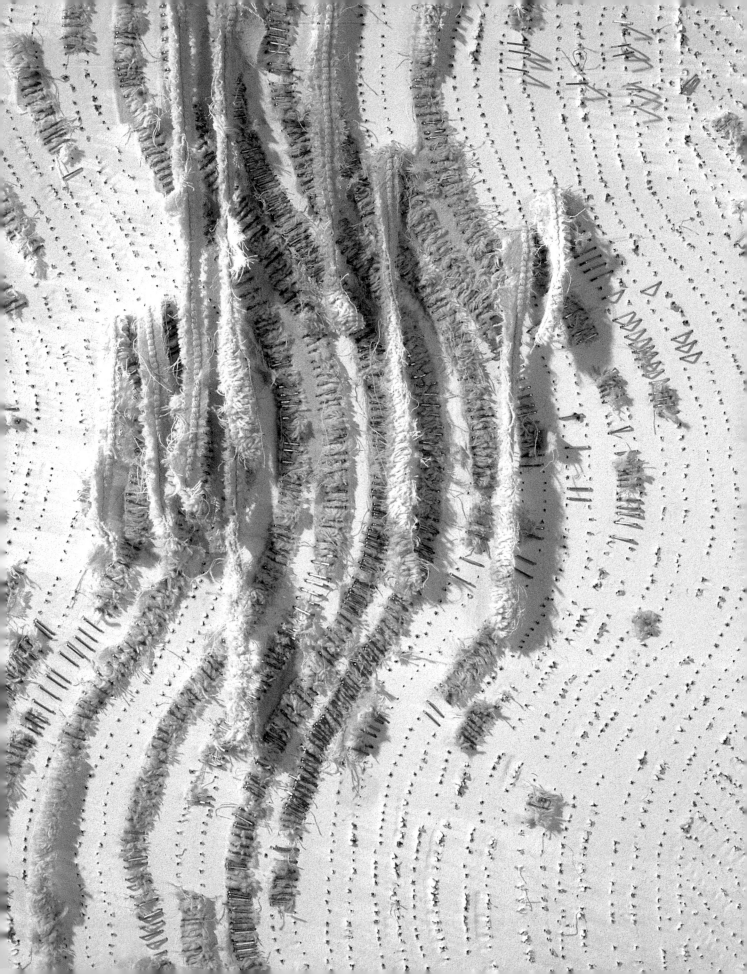

eugène van veldhoven

b. 1964 in Delft, the Netherlands;
lives in the Hague, the Netherlands
Education: B.A. (fashion design),
1993, Willem de Kooning Academy
of Art and Architecture,
Rotterdam, the Netherlands

Van Veldhoven utilizes a variety of new technologies to create his signature textile designs, which he sells to industry for mass production. Most of his fabrics are introduced as fabrics for interiors, such as wallpaper or curtains, although some are used in the automotive industry as upholstery, and others for haute couture. He creates about two hundred new designs every year, some of which are inspired by lace techniques and aesthetics. Van Veldhoven does not weave, knit, or employ traditional bobbin lace-making techniques, but instead uses the computer and his knowledge of industrial manufacturing techniques to design new textiles out of simple, pre-existing fabrics. He has explored hundreds of ways to manipulate, print, fold, burn, coat, and stitch in order to transform the selected fabrics into unique, original designs.

In the past, van Veldhoven incorporated lace into his work in a direct manner by appropriating actual lace fabric as a point of departure. In one example, he began with a beautiful floral lace and coated it with metal particles so it would corrode and become brownish-red, turning the delicate fabric into something rough, old, and ragged-looking. In another example, he coated an intricate, formal lace with the same reflective material used to illuminate traffic signs, transforming the luxurious, decorative fabric into a functional, pragmatic, "safe" design.

For this exhibition, van Veldhoven took a different approach by transforming seven plain fabric panels into designs that, as he says, "contain several strong propositions for contemporary lace, without using any lace technique." As an alternative, he created images that recall lace, "using faster and more modern production methods such as printing, burn-out, laser cutting, pleating, and machine embroidery." After selecting three unifying graphic motifs to employ as recurring elements in the series—flower, stripe, and lozenge (all frequently found in historical textile design)—van Veldhoven attempted to replicate on conventional flat fabric the texture, depth, and translucency inherent in lace.

For one of the panels, his solution was to develop two distinct repeat patterns, one based on semi-abstract orchid motifs, the other on a lozenge grid. The orchid pattern was printed at an extremely large scale, achieved by means of digital technology and industrial inkjet printers. The second, smaller pattern was created by hand using rotary printing, an older technology that restricts the scale of the repeat. By utilizing both technologies to print the different graphic images onto the same fabric, van Veldhoven created a third, even larger, combined repeat pattern. The resulting sense of textures and depth subtly allude to the visual qualities of lace without being wholly derivative. "Of course, by just scanning lace and printing it again, it turns out very flat. It's a superficial, stylistic, quick way of doing it. Now, I've found a way of making a new kind of lace by printing; and even though it's printed, it's never flat." Each panel in the series is equally inventive, and the formal relationships among the different designs produce an engaging sense of play in the series as a whole.

—J.S.E.

ABOVE LEFT: Van Veldhoven at his print workshop in the Hague, 2006

OPPOSITE: *Untitled*, 2006 (detail)
Burn-out print on cotton fabric laminated to polyester fa
13 ft. x 55 in. (4 m x 140 cm)
Collection of the artist

BELOW: *Untitled*, 2006 (detail)
Digital print on cotton fabric
13 ft. x 55 in. (4 m x 140 cm)
Collection of the artist

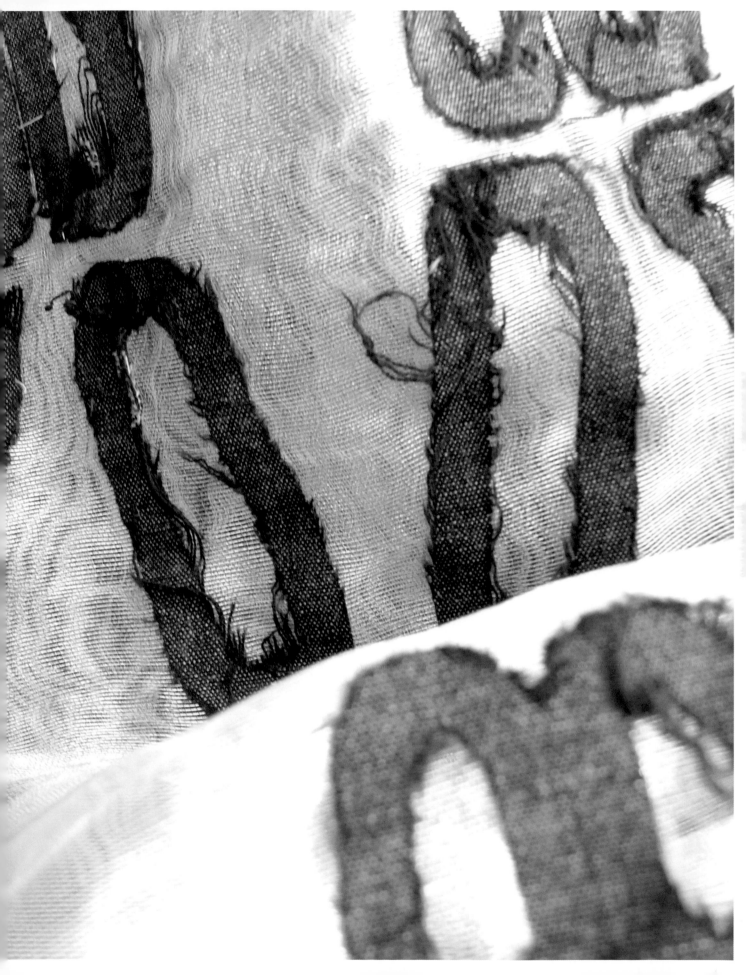

SITE: *Untitled*, 2003 (detail)
-out print on cotton fabric
nsions variable
ction of the artist

RIGHT: Installation view of *Untitled (Series)* at the
Gallery of the Royal College of Arts in the Hague,
the Netherlands, 2006

BELOW: *Untitled*, 2002 (detail)
Burn-out print on linen-polyester fabric
Dimensions variable
Collection of the artist

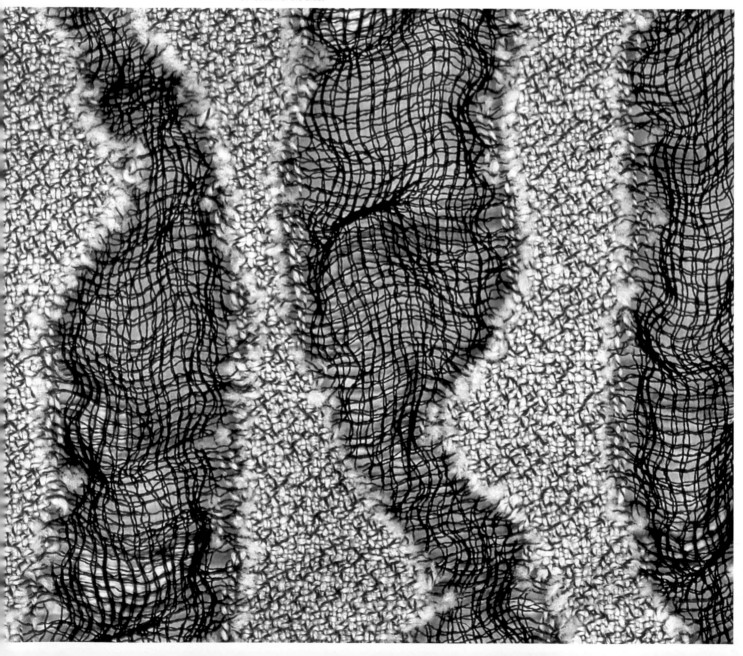

the beauty
of complexity

b. 1969 in Reykjavik, Iceland;

lives in Reykjavik

Education: Graduated 1989
(business and language diploma),
Commercial College of Iceland,
Reykjavik; B.F.A. (textiles), 1992,
Icelandic College of Arts and
Crafts; M.F.A. (new forms), 1997,
Pratt Institute, Brooklyn, New York

Bjarnadóttir and her sisters (she is one of triplets) learned to knit, crochet, and embroider at the age of five from their mother, an elementary-school knitting and sewing teacher. In Iceland, all boys and girls learn sewing, knitting, and woodworking in elementary school. "My mother taught in the winter and, in the summer, worked with us to develop new projects for the schoolchildren. From very early on, she would encourage us to discover new designs and develop our own patterns." Bjarnadóttir's early education in textiles also included numerous visits to art museums in Reykjavík. "At the time my mother took us to the museums, there were many textile biennials and triennials, so I thought that that these monumental museums were built around textiles—they were the art form most appreciated by everyone. But, of course, I realized later that textiles weren't considered to be that high on the list, and were even snubbed in certain circles." Since this realization, much of her work has been a reaction to that commonplace negative comparison of textiles to "fine art." Although she does not always employ textiles as her medium, they are a recurring subject in her art.

In several works resulting from her in-depth exploration of textiles, she utilized painter's canvas in an unconventional way. "It has been an invisible support for painting all these years, and now it will be the center of attention." For *Reconstructed Canvas II*, 2003, she took duck cloth (cotton painter's canvas) and unraveled it, reducing it to yarn, then used traditional crochet techniques to reconstruct the fibers into a deco

rative lace edge. By fixing it to a wall instead of draping it over a dining table, she makes a very clear statement about her personal esteem for the formal attributes of crocheted lace. In other explorations with canvas, as in *Gingham, Cadmium Red Medium*, 2005, Bjarnadóttir coated individual linen yarns with acrylic paint, and then hand-wove the colored yarns together with natural linen to create a gingham pattern. Affixed to wooden stretchers, the resulting "painting" is one that is embedded in the actual textile.

In *Doodling*, 2005, one of her works included in this exhibition, Bjarnadóttir has used drawing to reveal the automatic qualities associated with the rhythmic, nearly unconscious motion of the hands that occurs when making lace. Tatting, the portable and repetitive knotting technique she employed to make *Doodling*, can either follow an even geometric lace pattern or adopt a more open-ended approach. With white cotton yarn that she dyed with blue pen ink, Bjarnadóttir has created an organic "drawing" in much the same way we subconsciously "doodle" while preoccupied by thoughts or daydreams. The decorative, lacelike qualities in this work maintain a strong presence, which she unabashedly embraces: "I used to be afraid of people getting lost in the beauty of it, but now I trust that they will look further and find beauty in the concept also. Lace is never for lace's sake. It is a way to tell a story."
—J.S.E.

ABOVE LEFT: Bjarnadóttir working at a café in Selfoss, Iceland, 2006

OPPOSITE: *Untitled (Skulls)*, 1999
Crocheted cotton yarn, wood table
4 x 54 x 54 in. (10 x 137 x 137 cm)
Collection of the artist; courtesy Pulliam Deffenbaugh Gallery, Portland

BELOW: *Untitled (Skulls)*, 1999 (detail)

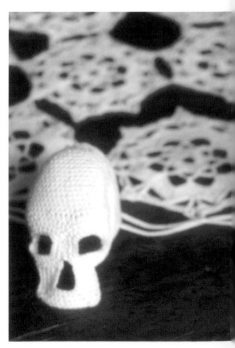

RIGHT: *Belgian Linen*, 2004
Crocheted Belgian linen
23 x 23 in. (58.4 x 58.4 cm)
Collection of the artist; courtesy Pulliam Deffenbaugh
 Gallery, Portland

BELOW: *Belgian Linen*, 2004 (detail)

RIGHT: *Reconstructed Canvas II*, 2003
Crocheted cotton (unraveled canvas)
50 x 21 in. (127 x 53.3 cm)
Private collection

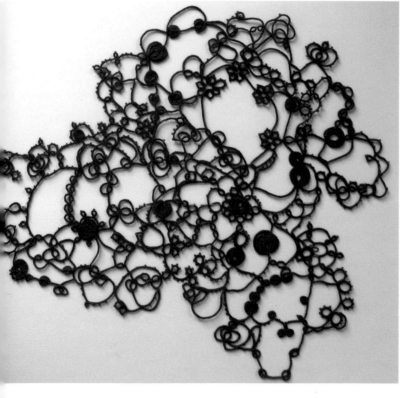

ng, 2005
cotton thread, red pen ink
5 in. (30 x 38 cm)
collection

carson fox

b. 1968 in Richmond, Virginia; lives in Brooklyn, New York

Education: M.F.A., 1999, Rutgers University, New Brunswick, New Jersey; B.F.A., 1996, University of Pennsylvania, Philadelphia; 1991, four-year studio certificate, Pennsylvania Academy of the Fine Arts, Philadelphia

Fox grew up in an environment conducive to art. Her father was an art historian at the University of Virginia, and there was a constant flow of artists and intellectuals at her childhood home. Most influential to her was Regina Perry, the first African-American woman to earn a Ph.D. in art history. "From floor to ceiling in Perry's house, literally in every square inch, she had this magnificent collection of African art and folk art. It was really beautiful. I was amazed by the work and by the obsessive quality that a lot of the folk art had."

Fox was attracted to folk art not only because of its obsessive character, but also its genesis as a response to particular kinds of need. Much of her own work has been about her response to death, expressed through memorials. Because of their relevance to folk art, the two forms of memorials that interested her most were roadside memorials of stacked flowers and candles, and Victorian mourning jewelry made from knotted hair of the deceased. Fox has used these cultural and time-specific forms of expression as inspiration to create therapeutic and obsessive works of art.

To make her memorials, Fox began studying handmade lace cuffs from the turn of the century that she collected when she was a teenager. In addition to analyzing the intricate structure of various patterns, she also considered "how this was a medium where women expressed themselves creatively; their frustrations and potentially their unhappiness were drawn in the lines of the lace." Inspired by the structure of lace and her musings about its makers, Fox used bobbin lace-making techniques to weave synthetic hair and wire into large-scale lacelike panels as a means of expressing grief. Beginning with direct, text-based works such as *I Know about Your Broken Heart*, 2004, her work evolved into panels of pure pattern that are infused with an undercurrent of horror. These *Hair Filigree* panels (one of which is in this exhibition) are made to look like lace woven from human hair, provoking a reaction of repulsion from many people, which Fox deliberately exploits to foster an atmosphere of unease.

In homage to roadside memorials, Fox takes a different approach. Using materials typically found on craft-store shelves, such as fake flowers, birds, and beads, she memorializes people she has known and certain personal characteristics that she would like to change. Initially, the works were covered with dirt or painted black to project a dark, heavy tone; but over time, the tone lightened visually and conceptually as she began to utilize elements of childhood fantasy to overcome her feelings of grief. In works such as *Pink Slut*, 2004, the pink glitter-covered text subtly emerges from the pink floral fantasy that surrounds it and, though sparkly and sugar-coated, "suggests something darker about the memorial or person it was made for." This series, like the *Hair Filigree* memorials, memorializes beauty and its passing, investing the works with a profoundly ghostly air.

—J.S.E.

ABOVE LEFT: Fox in her studio in Trenton, New Jersey, 200[

OPPOSITE: *Hair Filigree #3*, 2004 (detail)

BELOW: *Hair Filigree #3*, 2004
Wire
8 ft. 8 in. x 65 in. (2.6 m x 165.1 cm)
Courtesy Claire Oliver Gallery, New York

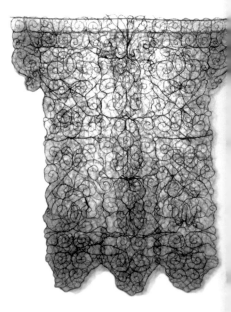

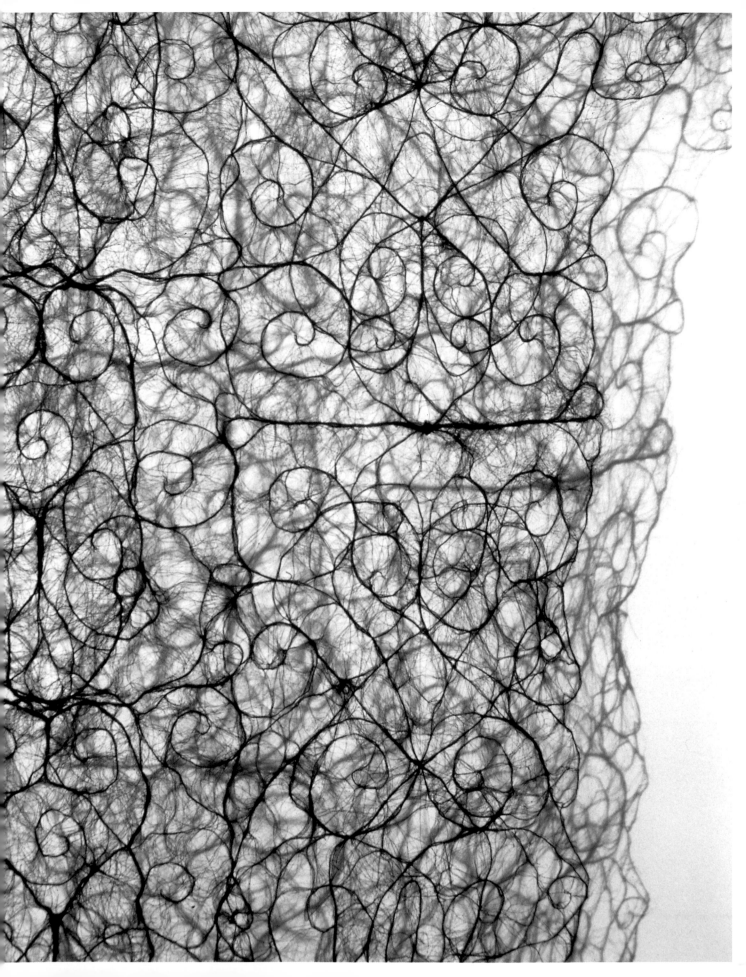

Pink Slut, 2004
Silk flowers, artificial birds and butterflies, glitter, enamel
  flour, wire base
30 x 32 in. (76.2 x 81.3 cm)
Courtesy Claire Oliver Gallery, New York

w About Your Broken Heart, 2004
synthetic hair
0 in. x 25 1/2 in. (2.7 m x 64.8 cm)
tion of Robert and Elizabeth Acosta-Lewis;
tesy Claire Oliver Gallery, New York

hilal sami hilal

Hilal became interested in handmade paper in the 1970s, and went to Japan twice (in 1981 and 1988) to study paper-making techniques. He went on to establish a department of paper arts and paper-making at his alma mater, the Universidad Federal do Espirito Santo in Vitória, Brazil. Ten years ago, Hilal left his teaching position to concentrate on his art full time.

Hilal's works in paper are handmade, using the cotton in old clothes that are given to him by friends and family—material that carries remnants, both physical and emotional, of a functional past. After he deconstructs, manipulates, and resurrects the recycled cotton fiber as paper, Hilal employs the new material to create delicate structures that evoke what he calls the "fragility and sensuality" of lace. Pigments and metal powders add color to parts of the work, causing a "patination" that often gives the paper a rusted, corroded appearance, thus reinforcing the idea of transformation over time.

Hilal also uses thin copper plates, corroding them with acid to create complex webbed patterns. In all his works, whether in paper or in metal, the "holes" are as important to the piece as the delicate lines and shapes that define them. He uses sharply contrasting materials and techniques in his explorations of positive and negative space, achieving an effect of solid matter transformed into something ephemeral, almost evanescent. Hilal addresses these contrasts in terms of methods and process: "The art makes use of two opposite procedures—construction (paper) and deconstruction (copper)—to obtain the same outcome: fragility, transparency, emptiness."

Many of his works incorporate text, either actual written words or a metaphorical evocation of them, but always highly ornamental, like medieval illuminated manuscripts or Islamic calligraphy (Hilal's family is Syrian). In these works, language becomes abstract, with real letters and words turned into decorative symbols, while meaningless curves and lines seem to form unknown letters in a strange, indecipherable alphabet. In some of them, paper and copper take the form of books with deconstructed sheets, the pages dissolved so that only the letters remain. In the work Hilal created for this exhibition, the book has become a series of veils or screens, with rows of letters repeated in three dimensions. The delicate three-dimensional lines become "labyrinthine paths" leading viewers across the surface, while the empty spaces—the focal points of Hilal's work—pull the viewers into the object space and force them to literally "read between the lines."

—J.S.

b. 1952 in Vitória, Espirito Santo, Brazil; lives in Vitória, Brazil

Education: B.A. (fine arts), 1976, Universidad Federal do Espirito Santo, Vitória, Brazil

ABOVE LEFT: Hilal in his studio in Vitória, 2001

OPPOSITE: *Untitled*, 2003 (detail)

BELOW: *Untitled*, 2003
Copper
12 x 11 x 2 in. (30 x 28 x 5 cm)
Private collection

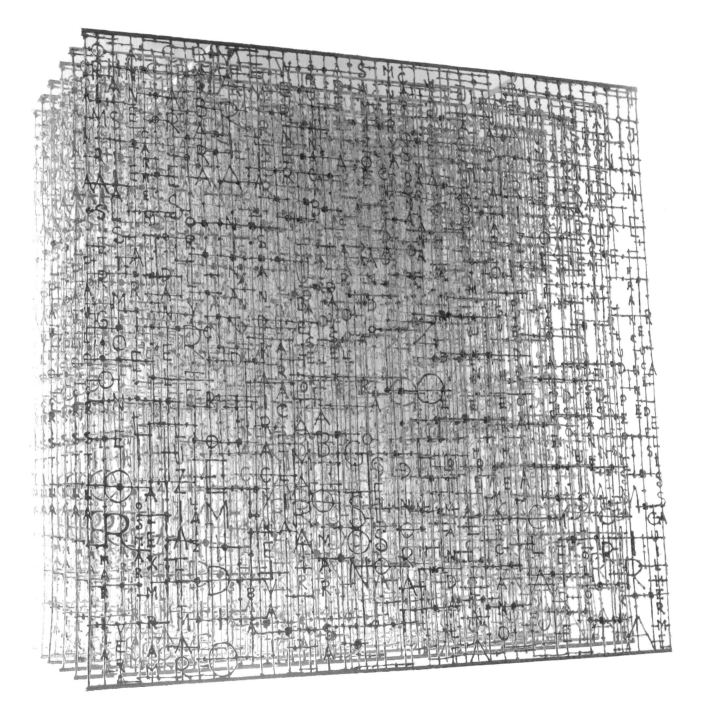

SITE: *Untitled*, 2005
n fiber, pigments
37 x 39 in. (170 x 170 x 100 cm)
ction of the artist

w: *Untitled*, 2005 (detail)

b. 1942 in Union, New Jersey;

lives in Delmar, New York

Education: B.A. (art), 1964, Brown
University, Providence, Rhode
Island; M.F.A. (sculpture), 1966,
University of Wisconsin, Madison

Mayer's installations are temporary monuments. Large in scale, they respond to the structure of the spaces they inhabit, creating their own internal architecture. Each work is formed of discrete parts that are only temporarily fixed together, often by visible ties. Mayer creates a uniform effect by keeping them primarily a single neutral color—usually white—that imparts the feeling of a monolith to the overall piece.

His interest in creating temporary structures began during a pivotal year in Italy teaching in the Tyler School of Art's study-abroad program. Seeing the layers of history in Rome, Mayer became intrigued by the process through which some things endured and others vanished. On his return to the U.S., he began a series of structures made out of wood lath. These installations were large enough to allow viewers to enter them and interact with them. The pieces of wood were not attached to each other, but were held together only through surface friction and the force of gravity.

Mayer eventually incorporated other components: shelving found at home-renovation stores and found objects from garage sales. These elements are arranged by Mayer on site, sometimes just stacked carefully and sometimes attached with zip ties that can be removed when the exhibition of the piece is over. Of his work, he says, "This is a structure that imposes itself and transforms an environment, but it doesn't permanently alter it; it is there, responding to preexisting elements in a particular space—I'm not taking down walls or permanently affixing anything. In other words, it has a light footprint on the space."

The objects in the installation are united by Mayer's interest in linearity. The elements form webs or matrices, creating lacelike patterns that shift as the viewer enters into the installation and his or her perspective changes. While the forms are often recognizable, allowing the viewer to connect with them more easily on one level, Mayer renders them neutral by wrapping them in white flagging tape (which, potentially, can be unwrapped at the end of an installation, as an extension of his emphasis on the "light footprint").

The installation that Mayer created for this exhibition is called *Drawing Over*, and it is related to two previous installations: *Drawing Out* (Zabriskie Gallery, New York, 2005) and *Drawing In* (Schick Art Gallery, Skidmore College, 2006). As he explains, the title of this installation "has several different meanings. One is climbing up and over: the other installations were in contained spaces that were all on one level, so they seemed to spread in and out, whereas this one, because of its vertical climb, will have a sense of going over and in and around things. It also refers to the idea of redrawing—a reference to my reusing preexisting objects drawn from my surroundings and reconfiguring the same components in successive installations. And it's a suggestion of redoing something, like a drawing, until one gets it right."

—J.S.

ABOVE LEFT: Mayer with his installation *Seventy Eight* a Hudson Valley Community College, Troy, New York, 20

OPPOSITE: *Drawing In*, 2006 (detail of installation view Schick Art Gallery, Skidmore College, Saratoga Spring New York)
Steel shelving, found objects, vinyl tape, wood, plastic Dimensions variable
Collection of the artist; courtesy Zabriskie Gallery, New

Line Dancer, 1995 (installation view at Alfred University,
 Alfred Station, New York)
Wood, found objects, vinyl tape, mixed media, metal fittings
Dimensions variable
Collection of the artist

OPPOSITE: *Drawing Out*, 2005 (installation view at
 Zabriskie Gallery, New York)
Coated steel shelving, found objects, vinyl tape, wood,
 plastic zip ties
Dimensions variable
Collection of the artist; courtesy Zabriskie Gallery, New Y

sheila pepe

b. 1959 in Morristown, New Jersey;

lives in Brooklyn, New York

Education: B.A., 1981, Albertus
Magnus College, New Haven,
Connecticut; B.F.A. (ceramics),
1983, Massachusetts College of
Art, Boston; studied blacksmithing,
1984, Haystack Mountain School
of Crafts, Deer Isle, Maine; studied
sculpture, 1994, Skowhegan
School of Painting and Sculpture,
Skowhegan, Maine; M.F.A, 1995,
School of the Museum of
Fine Arts, Tufts University, Boston

Influenced by Dadaist ideas, Pepe began working with readymades during her studies at the School of the Museum of Fine Arts, making automatic assemblages that she dubbed "Doppelgängers." Using a variety of found objects, including bits of crocheted lace, she created sculptural forms and lit them to cast unpredictable shadows on gallery walls, which she called "projection fields." Then, based on these shadows, she made automatic drawings on the walls, instantaneous linear impressions of what she perceived in those forms, engaging her imagination to suggest humorous, sometimes menacing characters.

Pepe, attracted to the physicality of sculpture and inspired by the linear qualities she had imposed on the "projection fields," began to "draw in space" with some of the same found objects she had used in her assemblages. The installations that followed the *Doppelgänger* series took the form of crocheted, knotted, and stretched lace-like sculptures dependent on and influenced by each piece's architectural frame and physical location. An early example of this—and the first work in which Pepe used crocheted lace exclusively—was *Josephine*, 2000, a portrait of her mother, in which she began experimenting with "making narratives from a particular family history in a particular place." Here, Pepe chose to work with inexpensive green and purple yarn because it evoked "the cliché of the traditional crocheted afghans that [her] mother used to make." The sculpture was installed at Thread Waxing Space in New York City in the winter of 2000, the same year she returned to New York after living in Boston for more than ten years.

Another work based on a locale related to her family history is *Under the F&G*, 2003, in which her grandfather's former shoe-repair business in Brooklyn and Manhattan is represented by crocheted and knotted shoelaces. In documenting her own family history, Pepe also makes connections to the general experience of the local population. Here, the crocheted, weblike sculpture was based on drawings she made of a section of the F and G subway lines' elevated tracks in Brooklyn, thus referring to the people who still use the subway to commute to their jobs every day.

Pepe is similarly influenced by location in *Midtown*, 2007, the site-specific installation she has created for this exhibition at the Museum of Arts & Design. The Museum is located among towering corporate headquarters and exclusive Fifth Avenue stores in midtown Manhattan, a neighborhood associated with business, commerce, and wealth. For her piece, Pepe has created a crocheted, lacelike structure using repetitive grids and spatial divisions that simulate the rectilinear masses and geometric order that dominate on the buildings and streets outside. The handspun, organic nature of her work introduces an element of randomness into the controlled landscape, evidence of the human element that operates within—and often against—its constructs. Using materials that denote femininity (such as tulle) and paying homage to a more humble economic past (as suggested by her inclusion of shoelaces and nautical towline), she challenges the visual and conceptual tenets embodied in midtown's architecture and the systems that operate there.

—J.S.E.

ABOVE LEFT: Pepe in her studio in Brooklyn, New York, 20

OPPOSITE: *Under the F & G*, 2003 (installation view at Visual Art Center, Richmond, Virginia)
Shoelaces, paint
Dimensions variable

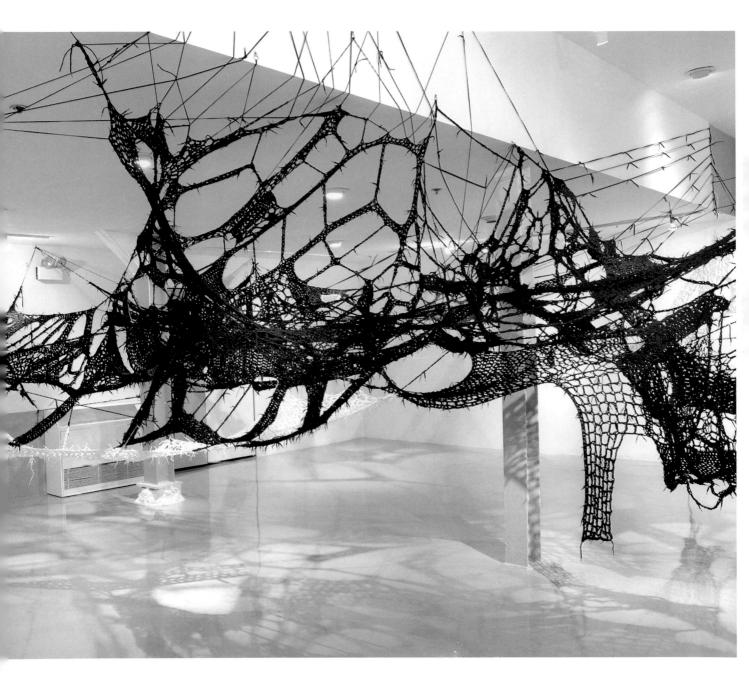

Mind the gap, 2005 (installation view at University Gallery,
University of Massachusetts, Amherst)
Shoelaces, nautical tow line, paint
8 x 10 x 60 ft. (2.4 x 3 x 18.2 m)

anne wilson

b. 1949, Detroit, Michigan;

lives in Evanston, Illinois

Education: B.F.A. (fiber), 1972,
Cranbrook Academy of Art,
Bloomfield Hills, Michigan; M.F.A.
(fiber), 1976, California College of
the Arts, Oakland, California

Wilson deconstructs found lace, eliminating most decorative elements to reveal its structure, teasing apart our cultural associations with lace. She then reconstructs the lace, restitching and knotting threads, and through display and association, re-creates meaning.

Although she had done some previous work using found lace, Wilson began working with lace extensively in *Topologies*, an ongoing work that she began in 2002 (and which was shown in the Whitney *Biennial* that year), made of various pieces of black lace, some from her family's cache of linens and the rest collected from all over the world. The work consists of fragments of lace that she cut out and, in many cases, took completely apart, then stuck with pins to a large, white horizontal surface to create an improvised composition: long motifs became twisting rivers or roads, bits of unraveled thread were re-raveled around pins, floral patterns were tossed into a big "compost pile." Wilson explains that the work developed according to certain themes: "biology, the connection that the lace had to organic form; urban sprawl, the way one thing is put down and relates to itself, and then something joins it because it has a certain dependency or need relationship to what's already been put down; and the openwork/network/connection idea of lace to the Internet, and the world of networked communications."

Wilson developed these ideas further in *Errant Behaviors*, 2004, a version of which is in this exhibition. *Topologies*, spread out on a large horizontal surface, made Wilson think of a movie set. She experimented with film techniques that would capture the feeling of the work, and eventually decided on stop-motion animation. "This kind of frame-by-frame, picture-by-picture, hand construction of animation is very much like the structural development of a piece of lace: both in stop-motion animation and in making a textile, the parts accumulate over time with sequences of motions that repeat and have the potential to replicate and expand infinitely." The resulting sound and video installation, first installed as two projections, consists of a series of short animated segments played in random order on each screen, accompanied by sound tracks by composer Shawn Decker.

Installed in a small room within the Museum, the newest iteration of *Errant Behaviors* is presented on two L.C.D. flat screens. A sensory stimulation of motion and sound present "relationships between humor and a darker aspect of content, evolving ideas about quirky growth, sometimes playful and sometimes sinister-seeming relationships, rude actions, repetitions and accumulations. The behaviors of *Errant Behaviors* have to do with aspects of impropriety, aggression, and accident."

The systems that fascinated Wilson in *Topologies* are no longer connected in *Errant Behaviors*; here, the reconstruction of loose threads and the re-creation of patterns must be done by the audience.

—J.S.

ABOVE LEFT: Anne Wilson working with students at the University Art Gallery, San Diego State University, Califor[n]i[a,] April 2003, installing one of the successive versions of [h]er ongoing work *Topologies*.

OPPOSITE: *Errant Behaviors*, 2004 (installation views at [...] Gallery, Indiana University)
Video and sound installation, edition of 8 (composer, Shawn Decker; animator, Cat Solen; postproduction animator and mastering, Daniel Torrente; copyright 20[...] Anne Wilson)
Dimensions variable
Collection of 21st Century Museum of Contemporary Ar[t,] Kanazawa, Japan; Lenore and Richard Niles; and priv[ate] collection; courtesy Rhona Hoffman Gallery, Chicago, a[nd] Paul Kotula Projects, Detroit

Topologies, begun 2002 (detail)
Lace, thread, cloth, insect pins, painted wood support
Dimensions variable
Courtesy Rhona Hoffman Gallery, Chicago, and Paul K●
 Projects, Detroit

OPPOSITE: *Topologies*, begun 2002 (detail)

Microcosm (One), 2005
Lace, thread, pins, wood support
5 x 40 x 13 in. (12.7 x 101.6 x 33 cm)
Collection of the 21st Century Museum of Contemporary
 Art, Kanazawa, Japan

Index of Artists and Exhibited Works

Page numbers for catalogue entries on the artists and their works are indicated in bold.

Photography Credits

BENNETT BATTAILE – Paul Hanua (photo of artist)/Bill Bachhuber (photos of works)

DROR BENSHETRIT – Geoff Hunt (photo of work)

HILDUR BJARNADÓTTIR – Hlynur Helgason (photo of artist)/Hildur Bjarnadóttir (photos of works)

DAVE COLE – Dave Cole (photo of artist)/photos of works: J. Carli (*The Knitting Machine*); Dave Cole (*Fiberglass Teddy Bear, The Money Dress*); J. Coleman (*Knit Lead Teddy Bear*)

LIZ COLLINS – Kim Stoddard (photo of artist)/photos of works: Dan Lecca (*Sock Monkey Bikini*); Karen Philippi (*Illuminated Veins [after EV], Vein Study, Pride*); Liz Collins (*Woodnymph Dress*)

ANNET COUWENBERG – Dan Meyers (photo of artist and photos of works)

FRANÇOISE DUPRÉ – Claire Bracken (photo of artist)/photos of works: Françoise Dupré (3 video stills from *Here and There, French Knitting, Fujaan*); FXP (*Fleur Bleue*); Noel Shaw (*French Knitting*)

JANET ECHELMAN – photographer unknown (photo of artist)/photos of works: João Ferrand (*She Changes*); Janet Echelman (*Trying to Hide with Your Tail in the Air*)

CARSON FOX – David Kelly (photo of artist)/Carson Fox (photos of works)

KATJA GRUIJTERS – Jonas de Witte (photos of work)

SABRINA GSCHWANDTNER – Kiriko Shirobayashi (photo of artist) / photos of works: courtesy Sculpture Center, Long Island City, New York (*Crochet Film*); Molly Virginia Smith (hand-made covers for *KnitKnit*, issue no. 1)

ELANA HERZOG – Richard Vito (photo of artist)/Cathy Carver (*Untitled #2*); Hermann Feldhaus (*Untitled*); Elana Herzog (*So Bennington; Untitled*, 2004 from the installation *Civilization and Its Discontents*)

HILAL SAMI HILAL – Sagrilo (photo of artist and photos of works)

YOSHIKI HISHINUMA – Yoshiki Hishinuma (photo of artist and photos of works)

CAL LANE – Paul Duncan (photo of artist)/Cal Lane (photos of works)

RUTH MARSHALL – courtesy Dam, Stuhltrager Gallery, Brooklyn, New York (photo of artist and photos of works)

EDWARD MAYER – Anthony Salamone (photo of artist)/photos of works: Edward Mayer (*Drawing In, Drawing Out, Line Dancer*)

CAT MAZZA – Zulma Aguiar (photo of artist)/Cat Mazza (photos of works)

ALTHEA MERBACK – Yara Ferreira Cluver (photo of artist)/photos of works: Louis N. Browning (*Picasso Cardigan, Ancient Greek Pullover, Ancient Egyptian Cardigan*); Althea Merback (*Ancient Greek Gloves*)

SHEILA PEPE – Bill Durgin (photo of artist)/photos of works: Cathy Carter (*After the Williamsburg Bridge*); Thom Kendall (*Mind the gap*); David Stover (*Under the F & G*)

FREDDIE ROBINS – Angus Leadley-Brown (photo of artist)/photos of works: Douglas Atfield (*Anyway, Craft Kills*); Colin Guillement (*It Sucks*)

PIPER SHEPARD – courtesy Baltimore Museum of Art (photo of artist)/Dan Meyers (photos of works)

NIELS VAN EIJK – Niels van Eijk (photo of artist)/Studio 4A/Peer van de Kruis (photos of works)

ERNA VAN SAMBEEK – Eric Dros (photo of artist)/photos of works: Claudi Crommelin (*Snow-cover*); Ilse Schrama (*Body Warmers for a Poor Family, Floral Gown*); scorselo&swart (*Turkish-Dutch Tulip Carpet*)

EUGÈNE VAN VELDHOVEN – Wout de Vringer (photo of artist)/Eugène van Veldhoven (*Untitled*); Nico Laan (*Untitled [Series]*)

SHANE WALTENER – Lupe Nunez (photo of artist)/photos of works: Lupe Nunez (*Knitting Piece #8 [London]*); Shane Waltener (*Chihuly Doily #1, Auntie Peggy Has Departed*)

ANNE WILSON – Severo Barreras (photo of artist)/Stephen Pitkin (photos of works)

HENK WOLVERS – Nick Kuijpers (photo of artist)/photos of works: Nick Kuijpers (*Lines I, Lines II*); Peter Cox (*Untitled*)

BARBARA ZUCKER – Ken Burris (photo of artist)/photos of works: Ken Burris (*Rosa Parks, Front of My Neck, Inuit Woman, Lilian's Face Flowing*); Ken Burris and Barbara Zucker (*Lilian*)

A number of the works in *Radical Lace & Subversive Knitting* were created especially for the exhibition. They can be seen in the following pages which document the installation as presented at the Museum of Arts & Design in New York City, from January 25 through June 17, 2007.

The work of three additional artists, Dror Benshetrit (Israel/United States), Katja Gruijters (The Netherlands), and Sheila Klein (United States) was not available at the time of the first printing of this catalogue. Their work can be seen on pages 154–155.

The Museum of Arts & Design would like to extend its appreciation for the generous support provided by the Mondriaan Foundation, Amsterdam; with additional support from Westminster Fibers.

Mondriaan Stichting
(Mondriaan Foundation)

WESTMINSTER
—FIBERS—

Installation photographs by Richard P. Goodbody, Inc.

OSITE:
ne Waltener
World Wide Web, 2007
ring elastic
nensions variable
ection of the artist

OW:
rina Gschwandtner
time Knitting Circle, 2007
chine knitted blankets, tablecloth, calendar, photo journal
ection of the artist

OPPOSITE:
Sheila Pepe
Midtown, 2007 (detail)
Shoelaces, nautical towline, tulle, metallic thread
11 ft. x 40 ft. x 24 in. (3.4 m x 12.2 m x 60 cm)

BELOW:
Edward Mayer
Drawing Over, 2007 (detail)
Steel shelving, found objects, vinyl tape, wood,
  plastic zip ties
Dimensions variable
Collection of the artist; courtesy Zabriskie Gallery,
  New York

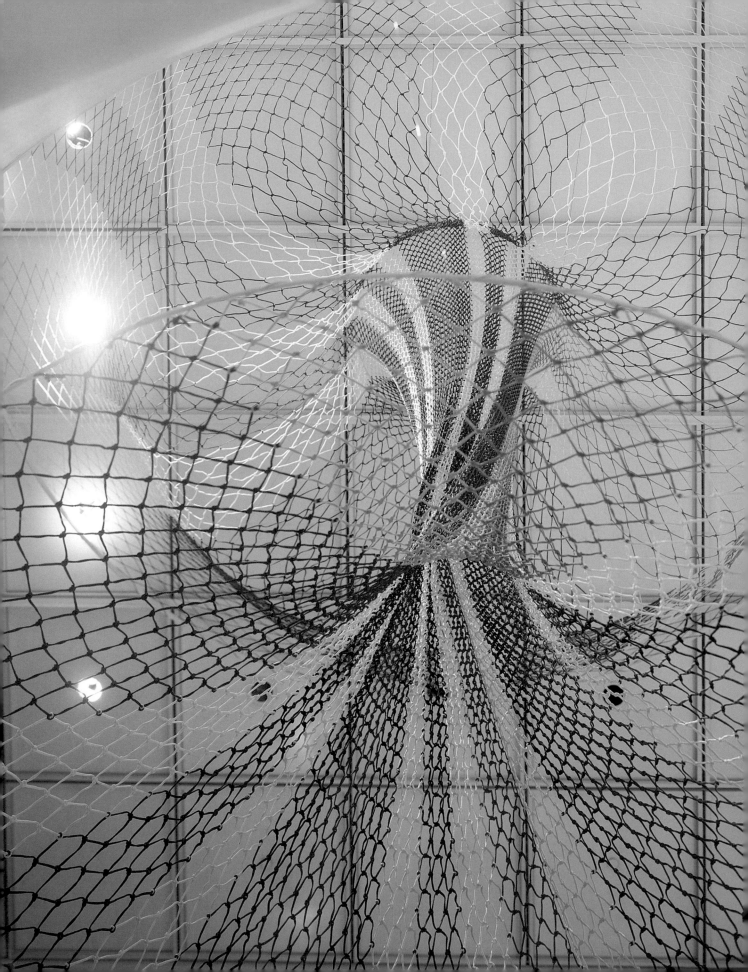

Cal Lane
Filigree Car Bombing, 2007
Found automobile parts, dirt
6 ft. 6 in. x 8 ft. x 9 ft. (2 x 2.4 x 2.7 m)
Collection of the artist; courtesy Foley Gallery, New York

OPPOSITE:
Piper Shepard
Lace Meander, 2006
Muslin, gesso, graphite, aluminum
Dimensions variable
Collection of the artist

Eugène van Veldhoven
Seven untitled textile prototypes, 2006
Digital ink-jet print and rotary burn-out print on cotton satin;
  laser cut wool stitched onto cotton satin, with burn-out
  print; digital ink-jet print on cotton satin stitched to silk
  organza, partially burnt out, partially cut away; cotton fabric
  partially laminated to polyester organza, partially burnt out;
  laser cut polyester satin; pleated, heat-set and laser cut
  polyester; burn-out print on coated, cotton satin
Dimensions variable
Courtesy of the designer

Liz Collins
Illuminated Veins (after EV), 2006
Silk organza, silk yarn, 3M Scotchlite reflective film
Dimensions variable
Collection of the artist

Sheila Klein
Cartouche, 2007
Stainless steel yarn, hemp, flax
7 ft. 8 in. x 6 ft. 8 in. (2.3 x 2 m)
Collection of the artist

Dror Benshetrit
Lily Lace Chair, 2006
Lace, canvas, metal, wood
42 x 30 x 32 in. (106.7 x 76.2 x
  81.3 cm)
Collection of the designer; produc[
courtesy of BBBemmebonacina,